CCTE Monographs and Special Publications

General Editor:
Ian Pringle

Directions and Misdirections in English Evaluation

Directions and Misdirections in English Evaluation

edited by Peter J. A. Evans

THE CANADIAN COUNCIL OF TEACHERS OF ENGLISH

13337969

9-89

ISBN 0-920472-06-0

The publication of this book was supported in part by
grants from the Pandora Trust.

Printed in Canada

TABLE OF CONTENTS

PREFACE vii

ISSUES IN ENGLISH EVALUATION: An Introductory Essay 1

PART ONE: LARGE SCALE ASSESSMENT 7

Michael Hayhoe: National Assessment in the U.K.:
A Brief Discussion of the Work of the
Assessment of Performance Unit 11

John Dixon: Alternatives to Mass Testing 18

Alan Purves: Opportunity to Learn: Evaluation and the
English Curriculum 22

Joyce Matheson: Large Scale Assessment in
British Columbia 26

PART TWO: ASSESSMENT OF READING AND LITERATURE 29

Michael Hayhoe: Reading and Literature 31

PART THREE:
ORACY: ASSESSMENT OF SPEAKING AND LISTENING 33

Michael Hayhoe: The Assessment of Oracy: A Report
with Observations on the Work of the
Language Monitoring Team of the APU
in the United Kingdom 35

Michael Hayhoe: Assessing Oracy 41
John Dixon: Four Ages of Assessing Spoken English 43

PART FOUR: STANDARDIZED TESTS AND ALTERNATIVES 47

Bill Allan: Trends in Educational Measurement:
A Publisher's Perspective 49

Bill Allan: The Use of Standardized Tests: 51

Bob Wilson: Standardized and Criterion-Referenced
Tests 52

Peter Evans: The Use and Abuse of
Standardized Tests 53

PART FIVE: WRITING ASSESSMENT 61

Garth Boomer: The Assessment of Writing 63

Andrew
Wilkinson: Writing Assessment: The Crediton
Project 65

Ken Watson and A Model for Evaluation
Brian Johnston: in the English Classroom 69

Hayden Leaman: Assessment and the Student 79

Hayden Leaman: An Analysis of Students' Writing 83

PART SIX: POST-SECONDARY ASSESSMENT IN ENGLISH 87

Peter Evans: Chairman's Remarks: The State of
Affairs (Ontario) 89

Roberta Camp: The Writing Folder in Post-Secondary
Assessment 91

Catharine Keech: Writing Modes and Writing
"Prompts" 100

John Dixon: Writing Modes and Student
Response at 17 + ... 105

WRAP UP 107

Bob Wilson: From the Measurement Perspective,
A Word 109

Sam Robinson: Afteword: A Reflective Reaction 111

APPENDIX: EVALUATION POLICY: CANADIAN COUNCIL
OF TEACHERS OF ENGLISH 117

PREFACE

The Canadian Council of Teachers of English, like its sister national organizations, has found it increasingly necessary to give special attention to a number of issues that have potentially great effect on the English teaching profession.

Evaluation is one such issue, and for several years the CCTE executive has included Directors-at-Large with a specific responsibility to study evaluation activities (especially large scale evaluation) and their impact, and to develop a policy concerning evaluation. As part of the inquiry, in each of the 1981, 1982, and 1983 annual conferences, CCTE organized major conference and pre-conference sessions around this topic, one feature of which has been the building of a network among those across Canada engaged in large-scale assessment activity.

At the 1982 Saskatoon Conference the possibility of an international conference on evaluation, with CCTE as host, was explored informally with representatives of the International Federation for the Teaching of English; it was proposed that this event occur just prior to or just after the 1983 CCTE conference in Montreal. At the next formal meeting of the IFTE executive (Washington, November 1983) it became clear that there was too little time to establish a participant list, write and circulate position papers, etc.; however, IFTE recommended that a less formal international session be organized as a pre-conference activity in Montreal. Members of the IFTE executive were also most helpful in suggesting presenters and resource persons from the member countries.

At the same meeting IFTE announced plans for a more formally organized series of international seminars, to be held prior to future annual conferences. The Montreal Preconference Seminar thus became a trial run for the IFTE series, and the CCTE executive approved publication of the Montreal preconference proceedings on evaluation.

Because the issue of evaluation affects so very deeply the teaching of English everywhere, we hope this collection of papers and presentations, both formal and informal, will be of interest and value at many levels across the profession, nationally and internationally.

I should like to acknowledge the cooperation of Mary Maguire and Irena Gerych, convenors of the CCTE Montreal Conference, both in making the physical arrangements for the preconference sessions and in identifying potential resource persons scheduled to make presentations during the main conference. From IFTE, Tony Adams and John Dixon (U.K.), Garth Boomer (Australia), John Maxwell (U.S.) and Ian Pringle (Canada)· were of great help in identifying and soliciting the participation of other resource persons.

Dr. Sam Robinson of the University of Saskatchewan, also a CCTE Director-at-Large: Evaluation, assisted in the Saskatchewan 1982 evaluation sessions and acted as co-chair of the preconference sessions in Montreal.

Finally, the many resource persons themselves deserve much thanks, not only for their formal presentations, but for their marvellous adaptability in chairing seminars, acting at short notice as resource persons on additional topics, and their general willingness to be in two places at once in an event far better attended than anyone had foreseen.

THE CONTEXT AND RESOURCE PERSONS

The preconference evaluation sessions in Montreal occurred over a two day period, and a number of the speakers at these sessions also made formal presentations on the theme of evaluation as part of the main conference program. Indeed, "evaluation" became an overlying motif for a good part of the week. A number of the formal conference papers related directly or indirectly to evaluation, some of them expansions of presentations in the preconference event, appear in Maguire and Paré's **Patterns of Development** (CCTE, 1985).

The first "preconference" day was devoted to a meeting of Canadians involved in large-scale assessment, chiefly at the provincial level, a continuation of meetings that had preceded the CCTE conferences in Vancouver (1981) and Saskatoon (1982). The main agenda item was "current status" reports from various provinces with discussion of problems and issues. This discussion was enhanced by the presence of visitors from other countries who reported formally or informally on large scale assessment in their settings and contributed to the general discussion of issues. One of these international reports, by Michael Hayhoe, **National Assessment in the U.K.: A Brief Discussion of the Work of the Assessment of Performance Unit,** is included in the present volume. And some of Bill Allan's remarks on standardized testing are carried forward from the first day into the report of the seminar on Standardized Testing.

The second pre-conference day was open to conference participants and organized as follows:

PANEL DISCUSSION: LARGE-SCALE ASSESSMENT

Chair: Martin O'Hara, McGill University, Montreal
Panelists: *John Dixon, U.K
                Garth Boomer, President, Australian Association
                for the Teaching of English
                *Alan Purves, U.S.A.
                *Joyce Matheson, Director, Learning Assessment
                Branch, British Columbia

MORNING AND AFTERNOON SEMINARS

LARGE SCALE WRITING ASSESSMENT

Chair: Iris McIntyre, Prince George, B.C. (Canada)
Resource: Rexford Brown, Education Commission for
                the States (U.S.)
                Alan Purves, University of Illinois (U.S.)
                Bryan Roberts, Dept. of Education, N.B. (Canada)
                Stanley Straw, University of Manitoba (Canada)

WRITING ASSESSMENT AND STUDENTS

Chair: Bryan Roberts, Dept. of Education,
                New Brunswick (Canada)
Resource: *Garth Boomer, President, AATE (Australia)
                *Hayden Leaman, University of New Brunswick (Can)
                Iris McIntyre, British Columbia (Canada)
                *Ken Watson, University of Sydney (Australia)
                *Andrew Wilkinson, University of East Anglia (U.K.)

STANDARDIZED TESTS AND ALTERNATIVES

Chair: Kathy Swenson, Dept. of Education, Nova Scotia
Resource: *Bill Allan, Sponsoring Editor, Measurement
                and Evaluation, Nelson Pubishers
                *Peter Evans, Ontario Institute for Studies
                in Education

* Included in this volume

Marjorie Hignett, Language Consultant, Manitoba
John Hutchins, Editor, Publications Branch,
Education Dept. of South Australia
*Bob Wilson, Faculty of Education,
Queen's University, Ontario

ASSESSMENT OF SPEAKING AND LISTENING

Chair: Joanne Bevis, Dept. of Education, Manitoba
*John Dixon (U.K.)
*Michael Hayhoe, University of East Anglia
Joyce Matheson, Ministry of Education (B.C.)
Emma Plattor, University of Calgary
Andrew Wilkinson, University of East Anglia

READING AND LITERATURE

Chair: Martin O'Hara, McGill University
Resource: Rexford Brown, Education Commission
for the States
Ian Hansen, University of Melbourne
*Michael Hayhoe, University of East Anglia
Alan Purves, University of Illinois

POST SECONDARY ASSESSMENT

Chair: Peter Evans, Ontario Institute for
Studies in Education
*Roberta Camp, Educational Testing
Service (U.S.)
*John Dixon (U.K.)
*Catharine Keech, San Francisco State
University (U.S.)

WRAP UP

Chair: Sam Robinson, University of Saskatchewan
*Bob Wilson, Queen's University

The opening panel established a number of themes that were echoed in the discussions within seminars throughout the first day, and re-echoed in the wrap-up session during which a report was received from each seminar. The same themes recurred throughout the conference — from the conference keynote speech that evening by Dr. Bernard Shapiro, Director of the Ontario Institute for Studies in Education, right through to John Dixon's reflections that closed the conference.

THE PAPERS AND PRESENTATIONS

Within several of the seminars, a number of the presentations were quite informal, and a good deal of time was given over to discussion of issues. These discussions were reported in

* Included in this volume

the wrap-up session, and I have incorporated some of these notes in introductions to the subsets of papers where appropriate. In a number of instances a resource person or speaker has provided me with a digest of his or her remarks, and I have drawn upon these wherever it appeared helpful in elaborating upon the discussion or clarifying the particular issues at stake.

Several of the presentations were formal papers, though delivery, especially in the panel discussion, deviated at times from the formal paper submitted. Again, I have tried to capture some of the less formal observations in my introductory remarks. Many presentations, though structured, were informal in style and in part responsive to a previous speaker. Some of these were captured on tape, and the transcript then reviewed and revised by the presenter. In this collection these retain their informal style.

It was unfortunate that the tape recorder failed us for Garth Boomer's presentation in the panel discussion and that he did not retain his notes. However, his basic views on the dangers of large scale assessment will be discernible in his later paper, "The Assessment of Writing".

There are two kinds of unevenness in this collection. First, because presentations varied greatly in their length and their degree of formality, some including "off the cuff" responses to a previous speaker or issue, the reader may be somewhat distracted by changes in tone and style. It was, however, impossible to edit and revise each contribution to produce a common style. Even had this been possible, a good deal of the flavour and sense of strong commitment and concern would have been lost. We hope the vigour of the exchanges will make up for inconsistency of style. And perhaps the urgency and importance of the issues will emerge better. Second, there are imbalances. The member countries of IFTE are unevenly represented, and New Zealand, unfortunately, is not represented at all. Nevertheless a good sense of "Where it's at" in various settings does come out clearly, even if the answers to all the dilemmas do not. Readers may observe as well that two or three persons appear to be "over-represented" here. That is unfortunate in the sense that it would have been wonderful to capture the less formal contributions of numerous other resource persons, too; on the other hand, those who do appear often were knowledgeable about areas (reading and oral language assessment particularly) where we as a profession have done all too little, and were immensely stimulating as well. Thus the one imbalance partly corrects what would otherwise have been a much more serious imbalance — virtual silence on aspects of language assessment — where most new work needs to be done.

The largest single topic in discussion was writing assessment. Besides the devotion of two seminars to aspects of this topic, much of the happier news being reported fell in this domain. Also, the seminar on Post-Secondary Assessment, given the interests and work of the speakers, focussed entirely on writing assessment. In an important respect, that was good news; it is encouraging to learn that resources are being deployed in this direction, with less and less reliance on machine-scored tests and editing exercises. On the other hand, the general situation is not yet as hopeful, certainly not in Canada or the United States, as these presentations might lead one to conclude. We have still a long way to go in convincing post-secondary institutions that the writing ability of students, in which they claim so much interest and about which they express so much concern, can be assessed only by examination of an adequate sample of actual writing, and that if it is considered essential to assess these students, it is also essential that it be done properly. Anyhow, the consequence for this volume is that it is weighted heavily towards writing assessment. Much more needs to be said concerning oral language, reading, and responding to literature than is conveyed here. For, of course, we do not want to convey a message that writing assessment is what counts and that other aspects of assessment are only marginal. The imbalance evident here probably reflects the imbalance in the state of the art; too little effective work is going forward in these other areas, or, if there is exciting news on these fronts, it is not getting around.

The organization of the collection follows roughly the order of events: first, the issues involved in large scale assessment as seen by the opening panelists, to which I have added Michael Hayhoe's specific analysis of practice of large scale assessment in the United Kingdom; then, the papers and discussion, organized topically, from the various seminars, followed by the observations from our "Wrap Up" speaker, Bob Wilson, who brings an important, and at least to English teachers, somewhat unfamiliar perspective on the dialogue. Within the topical arrangement I have set the all too brief reports on reading and oral language first so that they will not get buried, and then have inserted the standardized testing issue to stick out like the sore thumb it is; the remainder of the papers bear on writing assessment — the first group concerning writing at elementary/secondary levels of education (and these arranged from the "outside in"), and the second attuned to post-secondary, though practices proposed there are thoroughly relevant to all levels of education.

The preconference sessions did much to extend the network of people involved in and concerned about evaluation in English. I hope that this collection, a revisiting of the event, will reinforce the network, clarify concerns, and stimulate further discussion and investigation in many forums in many countries.

Ottawa, March 1985

Peter J.A. Evans
Director-at-Large: Evaluation
Canadian Council of Teachers
of English

ISSUES IN ENGLISH EVALUATION: AN INTRODUCTORY ESSAY

Peter J.A. Evans

I know a horse, a dog, a wench

- The Third Tempter in
Murder in the Cathedral

It is a very great temptation for the teacher of English to take the position "I know what's good for my students. . . I know good writing from bad. . . I want to be left alone away from 'the plotting parasites about the King' (or whatever other opprobrious characterization comes to mind concerning external evaluation)." And I think, behind the scenes, or as Sam Robinson says in his **Afterword,** during the beer sessions, many teachers do see large scale assessors and measurement specialists as parasitic. There is certainly a hostility, not a mere passivity, as Bob Wilson discovered, and a hint of his discomfort comes through in his courageously temperate "wrap up" presentation.

Robinson, in his "recollection in tranquility" of the Montreal conference, views the characteristic divorce between large scale assessment, with its often politically based driving mechanisms, and the world of pedagogy and the classroom, as the over-riding or perhaps undergirding issue, and sets out the need for greater cooperation and understanding between proponents of the two perspectives. While his perception is specifically a Canadian one, the divorce or potential divorce is a chronic problem internationally.

It is difficult to draw a simple map that adequately reflects from jurisdiction to jurisdiction the factors at work, or even all the "players" in this age of "accountability" as we look at the issue of assessment in English and particularly at large scale assessment.

Given that society at large demands and pays for schooling and that various segments or publics have interests, differing somewhat in emphasis, in the outcomes of schooling, how may these interests be legitimately addressed? When it comes to first language education, Everyman, or in these latter days, "Everyperson," knows a horse, a dog, a wench: the employer who claims student graduates can't spell, can't write a sentence, cannot present themselves coherently in the world of work; the interested parent who may not know or have much patience for theories of language acquisition but who sees the spelling mistakes, the untidy penmanship, the mechanical failures all too well; the hardbitten professor who never seems able to exhaust the list of competences his or her freshmen do not have. The English teaching profession has no shortage of experts at hand with free advice. On the other hand there are the teachers who also know not only a horse, a dog, and a wench, but more particularly their students, who feel under intense pressure from critics, and who, I think, feel in many cases a great deal of insecurity about the teaching of language: lots of theory, and seemingly competing theory, "out there," but a job to do **to-day.** Then there are the language theorists and researchers who "know," too, and who have a great deal to offer the teacher, if only the teacher would listen (and if only the reseachers could deliver their message in plain English). And there is another group, what I shall call the testing "industry," who have, at least, the skills to handicap horses, and who also appreciate profit margins; they have not only advice, but "solutions" — how to measure competence; how to "prove" gains; for the beleaguered teacher and school, how to get some of the monkeys off their backs. Finally, and sometimes both last and least, there are the clients themselves, the students. They have little say, and, understandably, not very much to say — but much to endure.

As for teachers at the classroom level, of them, it might be said too that silence and endurance is the best response. That is certainly how many teachers feel: variations on the theme of "Why don't you all go away and not bother me?" or, "If intrusion is inevitable, make it quick and clean and then get the hell out." Which may be the main reason teachers accept with few cavils the intrusion of commercial standardized tests and their scientifically derived scores — and either worship or ignore the latter.

The Montreal preconference seminar on evaluation in English addressed the fundamental question: How can one, in assessment and through assessment, respond appropriately and acceptably to these many different interests?

The responses provided revealed some deep divisions surrounding the question of publics and the "right" of intrusion; also provided were a number of imaginative and exciting routes to meaningful assessment, and at different levels, particularly in writing. Responses concerning oral language and reading in literature were much more tentative and exploratory; here, in those few reports and papers we have, the issue of intrusion came out most strongly: Can one intrude, and ought one to try to intrude, into the privacy of the reading act (Michael Hayhoe)? Though assessment of oral language is probably the most neglected aspect of assessment, is it possible to "intrude," to "overhear," without destroying dialogue or at least making the activity wholly inauthentic (Michael Hayhoe and John Dixon)? Both Hayhoe and Dixon see hopeful signs, but they are still a-borning.

Though it is evidently the case, at least in Canada, that commercial standardized tests are widespread, in most provinces this is a requirement at the system or school level rather than an imposition of the Ministry or Department of Education. They are, however, endemic and we find two interesting extremes: data religiously collected but little used to influence program though, if such data collection has a use at all, this should be it; and data collected and used, quite improperly given the statistical properties of all such tests, at the level of the individual student. I have remarked on this phenomenon at some length in my report, and will note here only that the present situation is professionally unacceptable: teachers and schools have no more right to use these blunt instruments to attempt fine-grained measurement than a doctor has to use an axe in place of a scalpel. Of course, doctors can't get away with using an axe, while many teachers and administrators believe somehow that these "instruments" are scientific, fair, and (blessedly) objective, and in that ignorance have convinced their local public that the school is really doing its job.

Bill Allan, from "the industry," issues some wise cautions which we should heed. He also admits that the industry, even with its statistical expertise, is unwilling to break new ground partly because of the cost and competition from other testing enterprises, and partly, I would add, because sales remain brisk. He also reports on a number of technological advances that will make "objective" testing more attractive. This led John Dixon, in his address winding up the general conference to declare:

> Ominously, there are also stories about teachers being
> evaluated by the tests, and schools. A publisher tells us
> that "cleaner statistics are being developed. There's
> virtually no limit to what can be done by machine scoring. . .
> The computer's future in testing is extremely optimistic."
> "For whom?" I ask myself.

Which is all to say that the industry will not stand still, and the English profession cannot afford to stand pat. We cannot afford to let the statisticians and measurement experts "do their thing" in what we pretend is a distant part of the universe, while we in our small corners do ours. It is high time we brought some of that cabbalistic science over to our side.

This excursion into standardized testing raises two issues of importance which, as I make a final review of the papers and discussion reported in this volume, received for the most part indirect or implicit treatment: the problem of validity and the issue of teacher education.

Concerning the first, I sense that it was taken for granted that assessment, however conducted and by whomever, must, in order to be valid, reflect the total curriculum. The "basic skills" approach most strongly represented by the standardized test and its typical item formats is an instance of very partial testing at best (the "at worst" I leave to the reader's imagination, or, if imagination is in short supply, to an item-by-item analysis of any popular test) with the implied message for teacher, student, and some publics that what is tested is what really matters. Thus a partial view becomes very rapidly a distorted view, and that distortion may have unlimited impact on teaching practice. Though in numerous individual sessions interesting aspects of validity were raised, the general or holistic view as such happened not to be: we seemed usually to be talking either of policy issues in general or of assessment "in" reading, "in" speaking, "in" writing, etc. Add it all up and one has an approximation of a holistic view of curriculum, but that may not be obvious at once.

Concerning the second issue, with the exception of references particularly in Ken Watson's and Hayden Leaman's papers to specific ways of coming at, of viewing, writing, not a great deal was said or implied about strategies for teacher education with respect to assessment: specialist teachers of English and Language Arts already well in harness, non-specialists who in these days of "student shortage" are being suddenly reassigned to English, and teachers in training. This is a shortcoming, both in the preconference seminar and in the world of education at large. Teachers under pressure, whether competent in English or not, are likely to respond to external threats to their territory in the manner I have already described, and in Garth Boomer's paper a strong case is made for the "Get out and stay out" reaction, though here it is the teacher who clearly does know what he or she is doing, with students who are also participants in the establishment of objectives.

On the other hand, there is evidence of gains on this front through large scale assessment, as reported by Joyce Matheson in the panel discussion. In British Columbia (and to various degrees elsewhere) a genuine effort has been made to "co-opt" the teaching profession in the planning and conducting of large scale assessment, and even in the reflection/reporting stage. The formal reports I have seen from B.C. and also from Manitoba on provincial writing assessment remain cantankerously large volumes chasing and reporting on far too much, but the design for participatory assessment has been good. And Matheson further reports that interest at the teacher and system level in the use of assessment resources and strategies developed at the provincial level has been very rich. Large scale assessment there turned out to be a "good thing" in that it got the teachers' attention. If that began as minute, focussed attention to the texture of the rope with which they thought they were being hanged, it has led, it appears, to a much higher quality of writing assessment at the level of the school and classroom.

The message is obvious: for all interested parties in assessment undertakings, there is every advantage in cooperative planning, in wide use of the talents of the professional teacher at all stages. Only in that way is there likely to be constructive change in assessment practice at the classroom level or worthwhile effect on program. The profession, then, need not hide out until it's over.

Among the specific issues more directly addressed were these:

Who are our publics?

In his panel presentation John Dixon argues persuasively that the public with a legitimate interest is the one adjacent to the school: the community and especially the parent. And he recommends imaginative ways of displaying and prizing student achievement at this very important level. The locus for assessment is the school and the classroom. Garth Boomer shifts the focus further, to "teacher and student," with the student sharing in decisions concerning writing and the writing program.

However, there are other publics who have a legitimate interest, the post-secondary institution clearly being one. It is of interest, therefore, to find Dixon, in the Post-Secondary Assessment seminar, reporting on his and Stratta's work at "17 + " to improve the quality of writing assessment, for the benefit of student and teacher certainly but also to provide a more adequate picture of writing performance for the information of that type of external public. And Roberta Camp's news in the same seminar that as august a measurement Mecca as ETS, responding to doubts about the adequacy of SAT scores, is looking, too, at the writing folder as, at least, a complement, is encouraging. And note here the cooperation with the teaching profession.

I have raised, in my opening remarks to the Post-Secondary seminar, a number of other issues concerned with evaluation at this level.

What is the English curriculum?

Though for the most part this as an issue of validity was dealt with at the margin of discussion, Alan Purves' presentation concerning "Opportunity to Learn" and especially his parenthetic remarks, reported in the introduction to Part One, raise one critical question and imply a second. If, first, a kind of external consensus is reached about what, as in the NAEP, a student **should** be able to do, there is a need to match that intelligently with the kinds of learning taking place within the classroom; otherwise, at best, external assessment will be a chronic series of misfires; at worst, as others regularly observe, there is severe danger of unfortunate skewing of curriculum. Second, especially for the first language, the question arises as to what is or ought to be within the school's control, as a formal part of the language curriculum ("opportunity to learn" in the school sense), and what kinds of learning, what aspects of language competence are largely independent of "schooling." Evidently, this is not a simple question, but the issue of evaluation requires us professionally to be a good deal clearer about what specifically we are to "teach" in a formal sense, what we are to "encourage" in the way of reading, writing, speaking and the numerous "survival" skills (in Ontario just now we are embroiled in a debate concerning a "Business English" Guideline — besides other interesting questions concerning it, **who** is to teach it?), and what features of language development, if any, do the school and the English teacher not have to accept responsibility for? Just who **is** responsible has bearing on the "Language across the Curriculum" issue, not discussed in the seminar. And the question certainly has a bearing on external assessment decisions, which may frequently be made without thoughtful attention to the question, with the consequence that teachers have great concern about the legitimacy and fairness of assessment, particularly as a potential reflection on their performance.

A particular illustration of the problem is **reading:** Is it the responsibility of the teacher of English or the province of the emerging reading specialist? This question received some airing in the Reading and Literature seminar, as reported in the introduction to Part Two. It needs a good deal more airing, for there is no doubt among outside publics that schools have the responsibility to teach reading and that reading proficiency, whatever specifically is meant by that, is a legitimate object of external assessment.

How can we improve the quality of assessment?

The importance of cooperation between the English profession directly and through its professional organizations and whoever is conducting external assessment, and the need for rapprochement between the profession and the measurement specialist are matters that come forward repeatedly in the following papers.

As well, the seminar presentations frequently addressed this question directly and provided helpful guidance. If the theme of the Standardized Testing seminar was negative (what not to do), the message of others was generally positive, emphasizing good practice. Even in the very preliminary exploration of "Oracy," Michael Hayhoe predicts that useful insights and practices are likely to emerge from the work of the Assessment of Performance Unit, and the list of tasks he provides gives a helpful push.

Many worthwhile recommendations were forthcoming concerning writing assessment: a model for classroom assessment (Watson and Johnson), looking past the writing to the student (Leaman), and the critical need, whatever the public, to report and to prize a sufficient range of writing achievement through the writing or "course work" folder (Camp and Dixon). The importance of student participation in establishing the goals of writing (Boomer) and in selection of writing and presentation of self (Camp, again) complement a perspective that sets the student, the ultimate client, at the centre. The challenge is to find ways of convincing all relevant publics that these are the best ways to encourage writing achievement and also to report it. And as Dixon notes, the missionary work must first occur at the level of the school.

Andrew Wilkinson, in denouncing more mechanical "counts," describes a means of expanding greatly our view of writing and writing development, complementing the types of study undertaken under other auspices by Dixon and Stratta, and alluded to all too briefly in John Dixon's presentation in the Post-Secondary seminar.

The issue of the validity of writing tasks assigned to students was raised tangentially in Boomer's paper: if students have no investment in the task assigned, is it a legitimate writing enterprise? See also Bob Wilson's rebuttal in his Wrap Up remarks. This issue was, moreover, central to Catharine Keech's presentation concerning the writing prompt, and her study with Leo Ruth of what we are assigning and how students interpret and respond to assignments deserves wide attention. The problem extends to our frequently inadequate definition of writing modes and expectations, a matter which Dixon and Stratta have also explored in depth in their recent studies. What both Keech and Wilson are suggesting through their research, I think, is that inauthentic writing is often the result of inauthentic stimuli and conditions under which they are administered: i.e. the fault may not originate with external assessors and assessment, but with ourselves.

The Montreal pre-conference seminar on evaluation responded not only to the challenges to the English profession in large scale assessment but also to practical methods for improving assessment and pedagogy at the classroom level. Indeed, if the profession hopes to influence in constructive ways the direction of large scale assessment, there is evidently need to **understand** more thoroughly practices in assessment at the classroom level, to **improve** them, and to **display** imaginatively for that immediate public — the parent and community — the quality of students' work.

PART ONE

Large-Scale Assessment

The following presentations, Michael Hayhoe's report and reflection on National Assessment in the United Kingdom given the day before at the invitational meeting and the reflections of three of the four panelists who opened the evaluation seminar, provide perspectives on a number of the major issues.

Hayhoe's paper focusses on the problem of the **authenticity** of, in particular, the writing and oral language tasks, extending modest praise to efforts of the Assessment of Performance Unit to come to grips with this problem in a context (light sampling, obviously tasks imposed *ab extero)* that in every way would seem to militate against genuineness, and alludes to some of the more imaginative tasks assigned. He also raises the important question of what performance in first language should include: not only "school" tasks, but evidence of ability to function in the world outside school. It would seem from his argument that it is both legitimate and desirable to make assessment more extensive than "school learning."

The three panel presentations are given here in the order in which they were originally presented. Unfortunately, Garth Boomer's paper was not retrievable. Alan Purves, from the perspective of the IEA study (macro-assessment at its ultimate), with observations also on the American National Assessment of Educational Progress, focusses, by contrast, on "opportunity to learn:" Should testing be thus limited? Or should it extend to what students "ought to have learned"? And how is a concensus on the latter to be reached? by implication, the whole issue of the potential or actual effect of assessment on curriculum is raised, if not resolved.

In an informal deviation from his formal text, transcribed from the tape recording of proceedings, Purves illustrated the "opportunity to learn" tug-of-war from what he described as "my personal historical view" of the NAEP:

The first assessment was begun in 1965. That year, almost eighteen years ago, was **Before Darkness** (B.D.). The goals were assessment in writing (which meant writing friendly letters), academic writing (writing kinds of essays that English teachers assigned), and, at the insistence of the president of the

German shoe company who was on the panel that set the goals, business writing. (He was a very wise and sensible person). The panel came up with sets of goals and tasks were created. The people who set the goals were leaders in the field. Many of them had not been in classrooms for a long time. They had all written textbooks and set goals on the basis of the textbooks they had written, and on the basis of a volume called **Freedom and Discipline in English.** In literature assessment, the same sorts of goals were set up: they dealt with knowledge of classics of literature, with the ability to analyze texts, and with some matters of preference. These goals were set by a group of people operating **a priori** from a set of ideals of what the American curriculum should be; it was that that was to be measured. The first assessment was actually carried out some three to four years after these goals were set, because there was a lengthy process of negotiation and change. Now the statements of ideals did not necessarily reflect what was going on in the schools. The panels had not surveyed the curriculum actually taught in classrooms. Needless to say, the children did not do particularly well, either with numbers or with descriptive portfolios.

But barely had this assessment been completed (in fact I think it was even before the results came out) when new panels came and set up new goals. These were "A.D." goals. The A.D. goals to a great extent repudiated the "B.D." goals, because the worlds of pedagogical ideologues had shifted. (This shift again bore little resemblance to what was really going on in the classroom). New sets of tests came out, including much more expressive writing and different approaches. And lo and behold the students didn't do very well again. The trouble with students in schools is that they don't read the **English Journal,** they don't go to NCTE and CCTE conventions and, further, most of their teachers don't either, and so they don't do any of these fine things. And they didn't do them very well on the tests.

The third assessment developed an even newer set of goals and objectives, this time much more related to schema theory and some of the reading and process theory. And again students didn't do particularly well in certain tasks. The only task in which the students did quite well, I think, was the early reading which was primarily a decoding type of test. That part of the curriculum has not changed in about 35 or 40 years. Because it has not changed, the assessment reflected the taught curriculum and so students indeed did quite well. What happened with National Assessment also happened with some of the state and local assessments. It also happens with some of the minimal competency tests: it happened in Florida where they found that 60% or 70% of the children at the end of high school failed the minimal competency mathematics examination, which consisted entirely of word problems. Then they went back and looked at the texts and found that the students' text-books didn't include any word problems and the students hadn't practised word problems. So, they didn't do very well on them.

The debate here extends clearly to what "the public" expects or demands as performance as distinguished from what is taught or not taught, for whatever reason, in schools. Thus, in the whole ambience of "accountability," one can move rather rapidly to the question of what teachers should be held accountable for.

The issue of **publics** or audiences for assessment comes out particularly strongly in the presentation by John Dixon that opened the panel, and it was strongly echoed in Garth Boomer's (lost) paper. Boomer stressed that, unless assessment supported the school's goal of deliberate learning, it was an intrusion that should not be tolerated by the teaching profession. His main theme was control: students also must have ownership of assessment; they must be collaborators in that ritual, and one challenge for teachers is how to permit students to share in decisions concerning what is to be learned. The issue of control or of power he later amplified with respect to writing in his paper on writing assessment (pp. xxx ff.)

John Dixon's "public," at least the only public that should matter, comprises the students, their extended family, and the neighbourhood. If **they** can take pride and joy in student accomplishments, who else has a legitimate interest? And the main thrust of his presentation is the illustration of how the legitimate right of information can be met, imaginatively and joyfully, especially through the display of student writing. Whether his answer is sufficient, whether there are not other publics paying the bills and other audiences (especially post-secondary) who students must satisfy, remains an issue, but the implementation of Dixon's suggestions could go a long way to meet the challenges (the negative) and to celebrate achievement (the positive).

Joyce Matheson, who clearly has had responsibilities, in particularly trying circumstances, to more remote "publics," views large-scale assessment, despite all its demons, as an opportunity for constructive impact on curriculum, and she reports very positively on British Columbia's assessment activity as an opportunity for resource development for teachers. With careful attention to teacher input in design of assessment and their involvement throughout, the outcomes of the activity **can** be positive, with teachers more knowledgeable and better equipped for teaching and assessing.

It is possible, and some would prefer, to see assessment as EITHER-OR: teaching ownership or "political" ownership — the former as "good" and the latter as "evil." The fact, in many educational settings to-day, is that assessment or the need for assessment is being pursued at the political level, and the challenge for the profession of English teaching is to influence that process in a constructive manner and turn it to positive effect. Purves illustrates the issue for curriculum; Dixon and Boomer illustrate the dangers (and Dixon outlines an imaginative counter-strategy); Hayhoe and Matheson give solid hopes for a reconciliation.

National Assessment in the U.K.:
A Brief Discussion of the Work
of the Assessment of Performance Unit

Michael Hayhoe
University of East Anglia

"English is in a particularly sensitive position. . .at the boundaries of school and out-of-school life, public and private experience."[1] And that brings me to the APU — heavily funded by the Department of Education and Science, seen by many as a monster of state centralism waiting in the wings to standardize education even further and remove teacher autonomy — and by some others as maybe the cavalry, still getting their act together on the other side of a couple of hills away, but coming over the hills in a few years' time, to help us all.

APU stands for Assessment of Performance Unit — a sinister sounding bunch. Who is assessing (whatever assessing may mean) whom (pupils? **teachers**?) — and why? and how? and who's going to do what with whatever they claim to have found out? to whom? why? how? when? Professor Harold Rosen leads the critics of the APU Language Team,[2] seeing it as well-intentioned but incompetent and potentially dangerous, with its foundation in a remit to do with unease and even dissatisfaction about "standards" — an ominous sign.

The APU was set up by the Department of Education and Science to develop assessment and monitoring techniques and use them in looking at standards of education in the United Kingdom. Work on language was sub-contracted to a monitoring team[3] formed at the National Foundation for Educational Research in 1975.

The APU Language Team has as its task the job of looking at general national performance at ages 11 and 15 in language — with language **seen as communication.** It hasn't managed to see language in quite the terms that Barnes and Seed presented it, in fact — a point I'll want to come back to later. Instead, it has tended to look at language as a **general school phenomenon** — not at English as a subject. That means it has been trying to devise tests which pick up skills which a whole school has responsibility for — and looking at some background variables (such as being Welsh or from the Midlands — but not at coming from a Commonwealth sub-culture) and at exploring the most fundamental of factors, that can't-help-it one of being male or female!

The Language Team is "steered" by a Steering Committee, made up of people from the Department of Education and Science, Her Majesty's Inspectorate, English advisers to Local Education Authorities, academic linguists — and two head teachers.

It also works with eight liaison committees of practising teachers from across the country. I get the impression of an increasing awareness of the liaison committees in reports and conversations — I hope that I am right.

The team is small and intense. Three of the present group have been teachers; all have qualifications in literature and/or linguistics. What interests me is its refusal to pick up anyone else's models or schemes of things and get on with applying them as they are. In spite of Bullock and the Steering Committee, it declined to use Barratt's taxonomy of reading and Britton's models of writing, for example. (It's to be hoped that some day we will have a **full** account from the team of why.) On the basis of its in-house and intergroup discussions, its belief that the old national tests were too narrow (they looked at comprehension in terms of slot tests) and its deeply held view that language is a co-operative process taking place in a linguistic and social context, it has gone ahead and done its own thing, devising its own assessment procedures and materials, seeking advice from itself, from trialling schools and its two committees, and finally carrying out the tests. The materials have had three basic "hopes" — that the language activities asked of the pupils should approximate to those encountered in school and, as far as possible, outside; that materials for reading and listening should come from discourse; that some assignments should cut across language modes.

The testing is intended to be done by "light sampling:" **some** pupils from **some** schools doing **some** of the tasks. The biggest national sample reaches towards seven thousand pupils, and there is a very strong anonymisation procedure so that nobody can ever track back to school or pupil. The tests themselves have been partly changed and developed as the five year testing programme has carried on — the result of the APU team itself finding out about possible techniques and identifying issues about language it wants to explore further as it has gone along. (This intuitive element makes me warm to it, if with caution.) Two thirds of the original banks of items remain in use for the purpose of comparison — but new items are introduced and the **scope** of the tasks is widening. There are more composite items. In writing, the team has started getting in samples of non-test writing chosen by the pupils themselves as their best work. It has begun to test oracy. However its two major limitations are unlikely to be totally removed. One is the inevitable component of secrecy in such monitoring, if items are to be re-used and teachers are not to teach to them (I'm not sure that they could, in fact). The second is the impossibility of the Bullock remit to assess communication in terms of "the demands made upon them /pupils/ in school **and likely to face them in normal life.**" (I like the implication there of school as not-normal life, but let that pass!) The APU team sometimes talks in those terms, but tends to talk of using reading materials which **pupils** would use. In the case of writing they have "tried to represent the types of writing work **generally undertaken in schools,** bearing in mind the purposes for which children of 11 and 15 may use writing." There's an unease there. Critics see that as a pressure to keep out of account **normal** language (if we accept that as the language of the normal world) and maybe the pupils' **own** language in those moments when, as Desmond Vowles points out, as their writing flares into urgent, important communication or intense reflection. The APU argues that this is not so. It will be interesting to see to what extent such writing does appear as the pupils' own choice in the current work-sampling exercise.

I want to look at the Primary (age 11) sampling, to see if it's a monster or not, bearing in mind that it increasingly uses tasks which employ more than one language mode and then does feature analysis and comments on feature interplay afterwards. So far there have been two Primary reports, a mix of fascination and boredom since they serve more than one purpose. The team is hopeful that money will be forthcoming to produce reports which focus in greater detail on the aspects of the work which may interest **teachers** — the samples of materials; of pupils' work; the team's commentaries on the examples; the team's criteria for assessment; the attitude questionnaires.

Let's look at writing first. In both years reported on so far, pupils received **one** of the ten assignment books for that year. All ten books had **one** task in common. All pupils had three tasks to do. All the writing was marked impressionistically; three tasks were subjected to detailed marking. (I'll come back to that later.) I won't go into detail. In fact, to do so would be impossible, since each report published so far gives only a **general** outline of **purposes** of writing and **types** of task assessed. For example, PURPOSE: To express feelings; TASK: response to a given poem; PURPOSE: to report; TASK; account of something learned. It does give actual examples of the three exposed to analytical marking. In the second report (1982) these were:

1. **PURPOSE:** To change the reader's mind/to persuade.
   TASK: Be a farmer/cook/teacher/social worker/prime minister/nurse/actress/miner and persuade the others you should not be the one to be thrown from the balloon.

   - testing - writing from a new point of view.
   - testing - writing for a new audience (knowledge of their real-life roles)
   - testing - writing with fictive components
   - testing - writing using conative skills.

2. **PURPOSE:** To explain and justify a personal choice.
   TASK: Choose between watching a favourite TV programme or reading a book which you like. Explain which was chosen and why, with enough detail.

3. **PURPOSE:** To narrate.
   TASK: Write an autobiographical episode - The earliest thing I can remember.

They found the first the most demanding; the second, less differentiating; the third, one that all could achieve — thus supporting teachers' intuitions. What is more, they explained **where** they thought the reasons for ease or difficulty lay, with samples of the work. Over four years of reporting, twelve tasks will have been assembled and made public out of the five years' testing. It is to be hoped that those will be made available, at least as discussion documents. Certainly, the team's own interest is commendable (and the tentativeness of that interest), as well as its trying to learn more about the relative difficulty of different tasks from the pupils' perspectives, and which aspects or components of the writing tasks pupils find it relatively easy or difficult to accomplish.

The problem, to my mind, lies in their not coming entirely into the open on the assessment itself. How, for example, are their impression markers trained? What devices are used to identify marker leniency/stringency? What are sub-features of their categories for analytical marking? Their categories are: content; organisation; appropriateness and style; knowledge of grammatical conventions; and knowledge of orthographic conventions.

I join others in seeing the first three of those as being very subjective and very large. I join others in wondering why the first two are assessed on the whole essay, the next two on the first twenty lines (how odd!), and the last on the first ten lines!

I would also like to know more. Which of those items involved other language skills? How open or structured were they — and how much was such specificity taken into account? (APU work on note-taking at secondary level has shown how much performance can be affected in such an activity by structuring, for example.) How far was the attempt to be "pretend-real" in the materials and the tasks successful?

The important thing is that pupils have at least written extended prose; have written at least some tasks they may have already encountered; may have met some that are new to them, such as editing for style and audience. They have not had to tick boxes or slot in ends of sentences. The tasks have had built into them that notion of **inherent tariff,** i.e. the pupil displaying his or her ability and his or her **style** of ability as well. It seems to me that APU has not been a villain and that it has done a great deal to carry out its remit "to produce national forms of assessment that do justice to the intuitive model of writing **acted on by most teachers."** [4]

Similarly, reading has moved a long way from the old slot tests. The team has devised for each year's testing eight to ten booklets, some with thematically linked materials plus content page and index. (Harold Rosen has attacked these for their lack of authenticity.) Some have taken "normal world" tasks, such as a holiday brochure; some have been complete short stories or poems — and so on. The constraints of assessment have meant exposing the pupils to the materials **within** these books and not beyond them. While the samples shown are interesting enough, they do raise the issue of how far they succeed in terms of Rowntree's "naturalistic" testing — suddenly having to work on whales, for example, may well not be the same as working on a genuine topic — and it seems sad that the "normal world's" reading materials are not more directly used. The team's aim is at least partly commendable in its hoping to produce over five years a range of years "reflecting something" of the variety of written sources pupils meet in school, in their own reading and for daily living. That "reflecting something" suggests a proper humility — but which skills they bring to bear and how they bring them to bear on their non-test reading need further investigation. It's good to understand that the team is using some assignments which involve collaboration, including collaborative discussion — perhaps their creation of more authentic "climates" for assessment is going to be one of their major moves.

That brings me, finally, to the work on oracy — that notoriously difficult area. This is based on the notion of collaborative, context-based, focused talk in which the pupils are **actively** engaged, within the test context. Again, there is no direct observation of talk in "normal life." As the team has gained confidence, it has been interesting to watch it work on task flowing into task, mode flowing into mode, for after-event analysis. It is also interesting to note that the computer may pick child A, but child A picks his or her own child B to work with, to avoid "communicative stress."[5] Let me give you a few examples of the tasks.

Jane observes an experiment with the teacher setting it up and carrying it out and describing the procedure as he goes. Jane then explains it all to Jim, who then sets it up according to Jane's instructions. Then they carry it out and try to work out why what happens happens.

Jane listens to the rules of a game, which the teacher "plays" — and then Jane teaches it to Jim.

Jane and Jim are handed pictures of a plant each; and each is given an illustrated sheet which contains explicit and embedded details of the plant and its need and virtues. Jane has to tell Jim about the pros and cons of his. They're then presented with pictorial and verbal details of an island and its climate and are asked to work out the relative merits of their plants as a crop on the island. One child writes down the results of their discussion; the other states them.

My own hunch, when I saw some of these, was to go home and poach them.

What is interesting is the assessment. The first stage is the teacher making global judgment on a seven point scale, checked on by a panel re-assessing the work from a recording. The interest, for me, comes in the analytical work on a sample. The team has a set of three general categories, such as SEQUENTIAL STRUCTURE[6] — but while that applies to all tasks, it is seen as having particular features in particular tasks — for example, description of a process is likely to be judged on a time logic; a narrative account may also have a time logic, but the possibility of stylistic variation has to be taken into account here. We are back to the old problem of the APU doing interesting work and not (at least, not yet) making its deliberations public.

Basically four general headings are used: Propositional Content, Sequential Structure, Lexico-Grammatical Features, and, fourth, a recognition of the realities of speech situations, a cluster of items which do affect judgment, such as hesitation phenomena; the extent of back-tracking, adjustment; factors relating to audibility and tempo. The important point to note is how the team arrived at these, for they are to do with **intuitions** and **impressions** which have been pooled — to arrive at what Mike Raleigh has called "informed opinion:"

The criteria are derived from the analysis of a large number of recordings of pupils performing the task in question. We HAVE WORKED BACKWARDS, as it were, from the impression marks awarded, selecting tapes exemplifing "good, bad and indifferent" scores to work out what were the specific qualities of the tapes that elicited the impression marks assigned.[7]

That work is still young. Its implications are several. The first is the valuing of impressions as starting points; the second the need to pool and discuss impressions; the third that such ways of working, in recognizing pupils as makers and co-makers of meaning, are expensive of time if not of money.

Some of the less patient are already seeing the APU as a way of shifting teachers — a move from its original attempt to monitor "ISNESS," to use its findings as a "SHOULDNESS" or even as a "MUSTNESS" device. My discussions with the APU language team suggest that they don't want any of those — that they are into the "MAYBENESS" game, and that they don't want to be brought out as monsters or as cavalry:

> Ultimately, we hope that the work will help to shed light on an issue which is of central concern to the research team and to most teachers. . .how far we do help pupils to develop their language for the many purposes it has to serve in their lives.[8]

It will be interesting to see whether the APU will be left to get on with the work that it wants to do and allowed to make its comments in its own good time — a long time span at that, with two more reports to come and then a quinquennial review. It will be interesting to see whether teachers continue to ignore it or, in some instances, suspect and despise it. It will be interesting to see whether the "16 plus" will insist on hauling at least some of its work out as an ally. In 1980, Brown pointed out that the APU's job is really to point out areas of interest for us to go on to ask more questions.

> If the programme leads to a serious, healthy curriculum debate, to funded follow-up research to improve what schools are doing, along with the necessary allocation of resources to them, the monitoring will have stimulated some worthwhile outcomes.[9]

Yes indeed.

Notes

1. Barnes, D. & Seed, J. (1981), **Seals of Approval: An Analysis of English at Sixteen Plus,** Leeds: School of Education, Leeds University.

2. Rosen, H. (1982), **The Language Monitors: A Critique of the APU Primary Survey Report 'Language Performance in Schools',** London: Tinga Tinga Press.

3. Information about the APU is available from Assessment of Performance Unit, Department of Education and Science, Elizabeth House, York Road, London, S.E.1. Summaries of its first four reports are free and give publication and price details of the fuller documents. Two look at primary school performance (11 year olds) and two at secondary school performance (15 year olds). No work has

been published yet (May 83) on oral performance.

'The Bullock Report', DES (1975), **A Language for Life,** London: HMSO had much to do with the climate in which the APU language team was set up. See especially Chapter 3.

4. Assessment of Performance Unit (1978), **Language Performance,** London: Department of Education & Science.

5. APU Language Monitoring Unit (undated paper), **The Scope of the Exercise.**

6. Ibid.

7. Ibid.

8. Gorman, T. (1981), **Language Assessment and Language Teaching: Innovation and Interaction,** paper presented at the Annual NFER Conference.

9. Brown, R. (1980), "A visit to the APU," **Journal of Curriculum Studies,** Vol. 12, No. 1.

Alternatives to Mass Testing

John Dixon

"Look, here, upon this picture, and on
this. . .like a mildewed ear
Blasting his wholesome brother."

1. Who are we assessing for?

According to the rhetoric of mass testing, it is "the public" who want and have a right to know. Who are "the public," we have a right to ask. After all, our business is to scrutinize language and the way it is used. I will argue that they are a political figment, and a convenient one, too, for politicians who want power over schools.

Schools and colleges **do** have public responsibilities, most immediately to students and their parents. How do they get a chance to judge what is going on? In my experience there are regular opportunities that an English department can offer students and their parents — and for that matter aunties and uncles, grandparents and the neighbours — to inspect what we are doing. There will be plays — even festivals of plays — where the quality of work in drama can be seen and compared with previous years. There will be regular "magazines" and publications (with some work of ephemeral, and some of lasting importance) which will offer a sample of what is going on in written work. And, more inclusive, there will be "open" days, with exhibitions and demonstrations all day of work in progress by all classes, and on occasion a chance for the visitors to join in and try the activities for themselves. This way people see the actual things that are going on; they become real audiences; readers and viewers for the end products of English lessons; and they can see and try out for themselves our pedagogic methods — using the occasion to learn and discuss why we have changed some of the old practices they grew up with.

What does this alternative imply? First, if you count in the students, their extended family, and **interested** neighbours, there is nobody left, so far as I can see, to the "public." It is shown to be a fiction. Second, this method allows people to evaluate the real thing: Students actually using language. Of course, it can be said that, for lay people, this can be very difficult (and so it is, quite often). But in that case , what does this tell us about the "judgements" they stand to make when confronted by mystifying tables of "scores" awarded to the school in a mass assessment league?

2. What are we supposed to be evaluating?

What students, parents, and neighbours want to know is often quite simple. Just to take writing for the moment, their first question is pretty certainly whether something **worth reading** is being produced: a personal or imaginary story; a poem or play to enjoy; or a piece of writing someone can be glad to read to get advice, information, instructions, explanations or a worthwhile argument.

If a student isn't producing a range of such writing over the year in secondary school, then "global judgement" ratings, "T-unit" counts, and "error analysis" scores are so much mumbo-jumbo covering up this elementary fact.

There is indeed a major problem with school writing today (and yesterday), so far as the U.K. is concerned, at least: most of it is "trivial," or simply "copying out" — these words come from recent reports.[1] For evidence that English departments are changing this long-established state of affairs, as some are, there is one sure method: inspection of a sample of the writing produced over a year or more. Similar kinds of sampling are needed to cover the uses of reading and oral communication.

I believe we can and should provide for parents and neighbours to carry out this kind of inspection regularly, as a group; to see whether, for example, students are producing things worth reading. Equally, teachers and consultants need to meet regularly to consider the same question professionally, in regional groups. And in parts of the U.K. this is happening already.

3. How does a profession report and share "standards" in English?

To date, it can be shown that statistical tables tell us little or nothing about what is achieved in a given piece of writing. The reason is simple: no count of linguistic features offers sure evidence of communicative effect. This should not really come as a surprise. Not everything can be counted or measured, and any good mathematician I have worked with has cheerfully acknowledged how abstract the things are that he or she can deal with effectively.

By comparison with mathematics, language is much more complex in the things it can describe and what it can say about them. You have to be pretty dumb to ignore that obvious fact — though some academics and administrators still do, admittedly.

Thus standards in written language (or in speech) can only be shared by selecting representative examples and analysing precisely what is being achieved, using **language** to make a complex report. This is already being done in parts of the U.K. When teachers do analyse achievements in writing, it turns out that certain developmental features in the **use** of language stand out quite sharply. (Thus, for instance, the story-teller begins to include inner events, or, in arguing, the student begins to take account of a reader who will not always agree.) As a result, it is not too difficult for teacher groups to select and agree on particular students' folders as "exemplars" of, in some cases, more elementary kinds of achievement, in others, more complex. There is close agreement, too, on the kinds of feature that are taken to be significant. (Equally, taking these features into account, teachers are able to diagnose tentatively what kinds of constraint may be affecting the writer at a given stage in drafting.)

As a result of experiments with this approach, we can confidently look forward to having such "exemplar" folders nationally available, together with detailed accounts of developmental features in the writing. This will be a vital breakthrough, because all exemplar folders, including the most elementary, will be made up of writing that is worth reading and taking an interest in. In the past this has never happened in public assessment systems in the U.K., and we fully expect a new, positive feedback on writing in school.

4. How do methods of assessing affect teachers and students?

Mass testing takes power away from teachers and their students, placing it in the hands of a tiny elite. It is that elite who determine, for example, what counts as a suitable sample of written English; what written tasks are deemed appropriate to thousands of youngsters; under what conditions the writing should be done; and what system of assessing (generally, scoring) should be adopted. This elite group then count as the "experts" on assessing, while teachers remain shut out as "novices."

However, fortunately for them, some teachers in the Eighties have already had experience of joint assessing and have come to recognize the range of expertise this demands — quite beyond that of the test expert, as it turns out. In addition, some of those teachers have begun to involve students in joint and self-evaluation. (Donald Graves has now demonstrated how six and seven year-olds can make a confident beginning.)

Which of these alternatives should be pursued and promoted? It seems inevitable that a system that leaves teachers as novice assessors rather than engaging them as professionals is going to have bad effects on their classroom practice. For, after all, assessment of some kind goes on in almost every school, week in, week out. Indeed, it is the delusions of so many of those weekly marks out of ten and percentage points that support the mass testing ethos.

In the U.K. at least, those "marks," "corrections" and "comments" which still persist on students' written work have little to recommend them. As teaching they are ineffective — an example of misplaced energy. As assessment they pretend to a precision (in numbers) they have no claim to, and accept an imprecision (in words) that betrays only too well the confusion and weakness of traditional practices in this field. "Good," "Not Bad," "Quite Fair," "Try harder" and so on: it is hardly surprising that such banalities have no direct effect on the student's use of language. [2]

Such practices, of course, are quite in keeping with the long tradition that for most students, writing is "trivial" and, more often than not, "regurgitation" of textbook or teacher's notes. But a breakthrough **has** been made during the last two decades, even though it may only have involved a minority of schools as yet.

The question, then, is whether in the next decade such schools are to become the majority. If they are, the financial and manpower resources at present being drawn into Mass Testing are needed for work on a different front. Every teacher of English should have the recurring opportunity to join in group assessment meetings, where the development of "a language for life" is traced in exemplar folders and (video) tapes. This is a professional necessity, and the national associations of English teachers have a major role to play. It is in this way that teachers learn standards (of expectations), simply because they and their students can **see** what might be hoped for — an actual piece of writing or speech. Ironically, by comparison, when it comes to such real standards, Mass Testing has nothing to offer.

Notes

1. Department of Education & Science (1979), **Aspects of Secondary Education** (London: HMSO), 81-86. Scottish Committee on Language Arts (1982), **Hand in Your Writing** (Edinburgh), 13-15.

2. **Aspects of Secondary Education,** 87-89.

Opportunity to Learn: Evaluation and the English Curriculum

Alan Purves
University of Illinois

One of the devils plaguing those concerned with student assessment beyond the classroom — and even in the classroom — is that which asks what scores on the various measures mean. During the 1960's in the United States there began the assessment movement that sought to say something about what students in general could or could not do. This assessment paralleled the cross-national assessments of the International Association for the Evaluation of Educational Achievement (IEA). There was one major difference. The National Assessment was, and is, designed **a priori** by groups of informed experts who met to decide what skills or content should be tested. The students either succeeded or failed on the various tasks. In the 1970's, the results showed that many students could not recognize many literary figures or works, had difficulty with metaphor, and with certain writing tasks. The only reaction was a wringing of hands, in part because no one knew quite what to do or why such should be the case.

The IEA studies differed in that they began with analysis of the curriculum, particularly published curriculum guides and textbooks. From these analyses certain areas were selected for testing because it was apparent that these areas were intended to be part of the school fare of every student. Some teachers were asked whether they taught the matters covered in the tests taken by their students. When the results were analyzed it appeared that one important school factor affected student achievement — opportunity to learn.

Opportunity to learn means that although students are supposed to cover a topic, they may not. The curriculum maker or the text-book writer may intend that a topic or a skill be taught. A teacher exercises judgment, however, and may or may not include the topic or the skill. In a subject like science, for example, geology may be recommended, but many students might not take it because teachers choose not to teach it. In English courses, an anthology may include **Julius Caesar,** but a teacher might not include it — so students in that class would probably not be able to say who Cassius is.

As far as reading and literature were concerned, the IEA studies found that many secondary school students in the United States had not had much or any opportunity to learn the following: reading of non-narrative prose; analysis of style and structure; reading of metaphoric symbolic fiction; analysis of imagery and literary devices; and evaluation of literary texts. All of these appear in curriculum guides and statements of objectives. Many questions concerning them appear in standardized tests, both commercial tests and tests such as university entrance tests.

We are currently undertaking an IEA study in composition, and I suspect that we will find "opportunity to learn" playing its part again. One suspicion I have is that American students have little opportunity to learn argument or reflective writing such as is typical in the academic essay.

Opportunity to learn is a troubling construct for those concerned with assessment or with the curriculum. It presents the dilemma that those concerned with assessment may justly claim, "Only teach what we measure;" those with the curriculum, "Only measure what we teach." Which is right? Is neither right? Let us explore these questions and this dilemma.

Those concerned with assessment could argue that they are operating from an idealistic position. In the first United States National Assessment, the objectives in composition dealt with personal writing (such as letters), business writing, and academic writing, and the Assessment found American students particularly lacking in the second category and in extended academic writing. Almost before the results were out, the Second Assessment was planned and those charged with setting the goals became enchanted by expressive and imaginative writing, and again the students fared only moderately well. The tenor of thought about writing in schools had changed. This change was heralded in the work of John Dixon and others and popularized in **The English Journal,** but there is ample evidence that the change was hardly actualized. Students and teachers were using texts and curricula of another era, not even that of the First Assessment.

In literature, a similar change took place. The First Assessment's goal included the ideals expressed in **Freedom and Discipline in English,** although there was some influence of the work of Louise Rosenblatt and a desire to include some measures that would describe how students responded to texts and what their attitudes towards literature might be. The goals included knowledge of past literature, particularly the Hellenic and the Hebraic, analysis and interpretation of texts, and a general liking of good literature. Again, barely had the Assessment been completed before a new group set forth a second set of goals which downplayed knowledge, and, to a lesser extent, analysis for a more generalized and affective response. Again this change reflected new ideals by a small group, rather than the actual practice of the schools. In the case of literature, however, the Second Assessment was not carried out until the end of the 70's and early 80's, with a new set of goals, more clearly tied to the thrust in cognitive psychology. Literature was then a part of reading.

In each case, the National Assessment was developed from a set of goals established by leaders in the field who reflected the latest thrusts in curriculum. This premise was, in effect, that what was to be measured was what students ought to be learning. It should surprise no one that most students did not do particularly well except that group of middle-class students who do well on most tests because they are adaptable and test-wise. But even they did not do well on some of the knowledge questions, just as students who took a 1940's commercial test on literary knowledge in the 1960's did poorly — "Old China" was no longer in the curriculum.

These tests — both the Assessment and the competency tests — were attacked by many concerned with the curriculum. The major charge was their unresponsiveness to what was thought to be the fare of the schools. Clearly many attacked the early emphasis on knowledge of literature and on business writing as being inappropriate to an "open," "expressive," "student-centered" curriculum. This same group also attacked the Assessment as an idea as well as behavioral objectives and accountability because all represented forces constraining their freedom to teach as they pleased and the freedom of students to learn what they wanted. In many cases, they attacked assessment in principle because they claimed that what the curriculum taught was unmeasurable. Tests were seen as narrow, limiting forces created by diabolic relatives of Big Brother who wanted to create 1984. The advocates of various new curricula used assessments as the antagonist when they sought to broadcast their ideas. Only a few argued that the so-called student-centered curricula might even improve students' scores on assessments, standardized tests, and competency tests. One might charge that realistically these critics were not student-centered but self-indulgent.

A serious issue remains: If assessment, curriculum, and instruction are divorced, students will not perform well on tests because they have not had the opportunity to learn. Students will be blamed, teachers will be blamed, society will be blamed, and occasionally, tests will be blamed.

To resolve this impasse one can choose several alternatives. An attractive alternative to some is to create a stable and sharply defined curriculum such as is done in several countries. Such a curriculum outlines the general goals of instruction, the types of selections to be read, the types of prose to be written. Assessment, therefore, can be calibrated to the curriculum, and lack of opportunity to learn marks a failure on the part of the teacher.

In such a system, of course, the curriculum can become stagnant unless there is a periodic review and reform, but the violent shifts that took place in the United States in the 60's and 70's could be avoided.

Another response would be to do away with national or even regional assessments, but I think it can be argued that such a step would only be folly. Assessments have the potential of acting as a countervailing force to the hegemony of textbooks. They have the potential of helping to assume that there is some commonality in the curricula of different localities so that students can move from one place to another with some sense of continuity. Assessments, finally, can show teachers better ways of measuring student progress. This last is one of the signal triumphs of the American, English, and Australian assessments which have been the cause of most of the advances in the scoring of compositions.

Those in charge of assessments should continue to refine their techniques, and in particular they should seek to provide a context for their results. The most meaningful context is one that is based on opportunity to learn as perceived by both the teacher and the student. One needs both, we have found, because the teacher's perception is not always the same as the student's. In New Zealand, we found the teacher to be presenting one critical approach to literature and the students another, presumably because the students were preparing for the university entrance examinations which the teachers did not like. Such disparities can be uncovered and should be illuminated in an assessment. Knowing about them may help teachers.

Assessment and research need not always be used to point up disparities and failures; they can be lights to illuminate success. Too often assessment and research studies show their authors' antagonism to teachers and seek to prove failures. As a result, teachers attack or dismiss research. This situation need not obtain. Teachers of literature in Sweden wanted to focus students' critical comments on the evaluation of the text. The IBA assessment showed that they had succeeded. I believe that similar indices of success can be found in many schools around the world. The point is, we have to have an adequate means for finding them. Opportunity to learn can help us.

Large Scale Assessment in British Columbia

Dr. Joyce Matheson
Director: Learning Assessment Branch
Ministry of Education, British Columbia

The continuing theme in Canadian literature is that of survival. In British Columbia when people say to me: "How are things going?" I say "I'm surviving," and that is a very positive statement in British Columbia this year. Large-scale assessment in British Columbia, in the way that I am using the term, is the testing of nearly all students at a number of grade levels and on different subjects on a sort of cyclical basis. These assessments are developed with a great deal of teacher input. Teachers are involved in developing curriculum in British Columbia; they are heavily involved in deciding on the objectives that will be measured in our assessment; they are involved in the development of the items which will be used to measure what has been learned; and they are also involved in the evaluation and interpretation of the final results, and in setting standards. And so I feel that in that mode there is a great deal of teacher input, a great deal of teacher understanding, and an incredible amount of teacher learning that goes on through these processes. Moreover, as we do them year after year, more and more people get involved.

One of our major concerns in all assessments, but particularly in language arts, is that we feel that the wisdom that has been developed through the last few years is taking a long time, for those of us who are impatient, to get down to every teacher in every classroom. So one of our basic aims has always been to help improve the quality of teaching and the quality of assessment within the individual classroom. What comes out of assessment is related to that: basically, we say that assessment is undertaken so that better decisions will be made in the school. That is essential.

For example, out of our assessments come instructional materials. We have what we call "the boxes" in British Columbia — they are about 6 centimetres thick, one for elementary and one for secondary, based on the materials that were developed for assessment of written expression several years ago. These were made available to the schools: they give samples of the kinds of questions that were asked, and lists of the scales that were used to evaluate. We're saying, "Hey, teachers, this is the way we assess, this is the way we marked when we did assess. How would you like to try some of these methods and see how they work in your classroom?'' Thus we try to connect what we're doing to what we think teachers should be doing.

Recently, a new writing program was introduced, and the Assessment Branch was quite concerned because, according to the way the regulations read, the principal of the Junior High School had to decide which students would be required to take the writing course in Grade 11. We felt that some principals might have a little trouble evaluating writing in order to make that decision. Accordingly, we decided to develop an "evaluation of writing" kit, which appears now to have received the name **Writing Evaluation Folio,** or WEF. (We thought "folio" was a nice word in English.) In developing the folio we created one section on English (which was fairly logical), but we also created a section on writing in science and another on writing in social studies. This went out to the field. Some teachers have picked it up, run with it, and think it's marvellous; others don't know it exists, which is typical for Ministry-developed material. However, it was very heartening, when the High School Science Curriculum was being developed and a guide being put out, that the developers asked if the materials on writing in science could be included as part of that guide. I thought that was a healthy outcome for assessment activity.

Another thing that we have done is to develop classroom achievement tests, as have a number of other provinces in Canada. We develop good assessment instruments, and then encourage teachers to use some ways of marking that are not merely error counting, or stressing the negative parts of what students are doing, but rather showing what the criteria are, how the essays are being marked, and consequently letting teachers see how they can improve their own marking.

We're also interested in consultation with School Districts, and in talking to teachers in various districts on assessment matters in all fields. Several districts concerned about writing evaluation initiated their own projects. One of the most successful of these was called **The Young Writer's Project.** In this program, writing is taught as process. Recently, the Ministry published the package for a workshop on this project, and included in them is a section on the evaluation of writing. Now, since the first written assessment, all of the material that has come from the government, including the evaluation sections in curriculum, has had the same themes; they have all had the same ideas; they have all believed in the same philosophy of writing. That has been healthy and there has been a lot of learning. People have been put in the situation that new Ministry materials support and affirm what they have begun to do on the advice of earlier Ministry materials.

We are also looking at listening and speaking. We are considering doing an assessment of them, but a teacher came up to me one day and said, "I don't think you should do an assessment of listening and speaking when you haven't told us what to do, how to do it, or how to measure it." And so we are going to try to start the other way around. We shall first develop some tests of listening and put them out in the field with the challenge: "Try them. See how they work." And then we are going to do the assessment a little later when teachers are more comfortable with the kind of things that we would like them to do.

I would like to touch for a moment on what someone in my office once referred to as capitalizing on catastrophe. (I think this is a characteristic Canadian attitude, so I felt it fit in here.) We have had some trouble in large scale assessment in British Columbia recently. We have had, in our eyes, gross misuse of assessment results: The publication of district by district results and comments made about "good" and "bad" districts. Added to that was the mandating of final examinations. According to the original statement, it looked as if there were going to be final examinations in every subject, for every student, at every grade level, and that we were going to evaluate student learning, teacher competence, school success and district effects all at once. The Learning Assessment Branch is not a comfortable place to be with that kind of talk going on, because we know that you cannot use one test to measure all these different things.

But the final result is that we now do have mandatory tests. They are teacher marked. We are providing norms and standards with them. We have standard-setting committees of teachers look at the test, do the questions, and say, "All right, what is a good standard of achievement on this particular test?" and then we send that out to the districts. We are testing mathematics in grade 3, 7 to 10, reading at grades 4 and 7, and algebra, chemistry and writing at grade 12.

In the grade 4 and 7 reading tests, we test only comprehension. On one scale of the table of specifications, we have **Words, Sentences, Paragraphs,** and **Multi-Paragraphs,** and across the top we have the levels **(Literal, Inferential,** and **Beyond Inferential.)** We are trying to measure in that way. When I talked to some school districts about this, a man came up to me afterwards and asked, "Are you measuring comprehension at grade 4?" I said, "Yes." Then he said, "But we don't teach comprehension until the beginning of grade 4. We teach decoding skills, we teach phonics, we teach . . . . What do you mean by measuring comprehension?" It was then that I became aware that maybe what we set out to do in 1983 will have some good effects out there. Maybe we are capitalizing on catastrophe. There still are people out there who think that there is something other than comprehension in reading. This is the kind of influence we can have.

For grade 12 Writing, we put out a 24 page booklet — the Teacher's Manual - which is really a bit of propaganda on our part. When the test was designed, we decided that we would only measure actual student writing. We would not do any multiple-choice tests on grammar or punctuation. We had said that we only wanted this exam to last one hour. There are some problems in that: we felt that if we had a test that lasted for two or three hours and said, "But it should only count a little bit," we would only run into problems, especially when it is mandated. So we said, "All right. We're only going to allow students one hour, but that will mean that this will really be a first draft." And we emphasize that it should be marked from that standpoint, and that the marking should be able to be done in ten minutes per paper. We have included a whole section on how the writing is to be marked using the scales. We suggest that, as it is only one piece of writing, it is not a fair way to evaluate students' writing; therefore, we expect teachers will have looked at a lot of other student material. And we list the minimum and maximum amounts that we would expect this test to count toward any final mark. We recommend between ten and twenty-five percent of the writing strand, which gives districts a lot of leeway.

So I think that all of us are going to have to look more closely at assessment. Though we are all concerned about associating the term "evaluation" with writing, the more that we can spread the message from the wisdom that we have gained in the last little while, the better off we'll be.

Part Two

Assessment of Reading and Literature

From the summary notes from this seminar, the dialogue in this session appears to have been at times vigorous, irreverent, concerning current practices, and at times filled with a quiet, reverent hush concerning the **privacy** of the reading act, this last best illustrated by the one short paper by Michael Hayhoe that emerged intact.

The privacy of the reading act was an issue strongly stated by Ian Hansen who kindly forwarded a digest of his remarks from which I quote:

> There has been, I believe, a decline in what St. Augustine called "reading with unmoving lips." What was a private activity has given place to a communal one of public import. After nearly twenty years, the growth model of English teaching (**pace** John Dixon) is still being misinterpreted by classroom teachers as a public enterprise. As George Steiner has observed: "The bias of current sentiment points insistently towards gregariousness." The act of reading is profoundly solitary. We listen to books in our own room, as it were . . . For the young reader, the mental silence after that last page is most important in the reading, a point made by Michael Hayhoe in his paper.
>
> It is being still in one's room that is an element missing in the organised amnesia of our schools. I make a plea, therefore, for personal and private "meanings." We must stop bullying our students into reading collectivism. And that means we have to read a great deal more than we do. We have to be confident and courageous enough to let our students read on their own. Young people must assess themselves: they put up the test in their own room, testing themselves against the book. We forget that strategy at our own and our students' peril.

Much of the discussion in this session concerned dichotomies — between private and public in pursuit of the questions raised by Ian Hansen and by Michael Hayhoe in the following brief paper, and between "Reading" and the specialist interest in reading over against reading in the English program. Martin O'Hara, chairperson of the seminar, reported the "American" anomaly of "a reading profession which is somehow divorced from the teaching of literature" and the difficulties and disputes that have followed from that over, for example, what constitutes "reading comprehension". In his summary he quoted from Alan Purves' remarks during the seminar:

> Does literature belong in the school now that we have reading and writing? Where is the locus? Is it in development or in schooling? Where is the locus of meaning? Is it in the text or in the reader?

This last question is taken up in the Hayhoe paper. The debate, for the group and for the profession is well summarized in the recollection Alan Purves sent to me following the conference: he saw literature as:

> caught between reading and writing, both of which were in vogue; literature's assessment being caught between the text and the reader, between meaning and significance, between the public and the private, between the approved response and the personal response. Assessment therefore becomes a balancing act, which we agreed was not an easy task, but all the balancing matched the balancing that must take place in the curriculum and the classroom.

Though this seminar did not reach a consensus or provide recommendations, it set out some of the critical issues in a manner that may serve others as a starting point for their resolution.

Reading and Literature

M.J. Hayhoe
University of East Anglia

There is a poem by Charles Causley called **Timothy Winters.** Timothy is a "blitz
of a boy," lives in a slum with his gin-sotted granny, is "ineducable."
  The end of the poem runs:

> At Morning Prayers the Master helves
> For children less fortunate than ourselves,
> And the loudest response in the room is when
> Timothy Winters roars "Amen!"
>
> So come one angel, come on ten:
> Timothy Winters says "Amen
> Amen amen amen amen.
> **Timothy Winters, Lord.**

Amen"

  I once read that poem at a words and music evening — or, if you like, that
poem read me. And so, when I came to the end, the poem came out full of
energy, young Tim unaware of his misery, cocky and belligerent, a life force
which would not be put down.
  And when my colleague Peter Miller read the same poem a year later at the
same event, his hands sank to his side as his voice moved from Timothy's un-
couth shouting "Amen!" to a quietening, half-despairing, half-accusing turning
to God — with a long silence — and a final "Amen" which could be barely heard
and was totally ambiguous, a question mark probing each listener.
  I've told that rather long anecdote since it is an important one in my life and
since it raises the basic issue of how we assess what is happening when, to quote
Barbara Ward, we bring our lives to books and have our lives affected by them.
Behind that is another issue: what forms of "assessment" are morally tolerable?

If we accept Heraclitus that no man steps in the same stream twice — the stream has changed and **so has the man;** if we accept Eliot's dictum that the pattern is "new and shocking" in every moment; if we accept that experience of literature is at least partly holistic, affective and not to be pinned down, we face serious challenges when we decide to go ahead with assessing and when we decide upon our assessment devices.

Assessment of "basic literacy" goes on in British education, as it should, with a variety of testing devices. Assessment of literacy in literature has largely been the province of the examinations which signify the end of compulsory education at 16. These have tended to take two directions.

The first, for the more able pupils, has been the "law court" game: being assigned a task and asked to appear as counsel for the defence or prosecution. "Is Lady Macbeth totally evil? Discuss" leads to the candidate adopting an appropriate detached style in which assertions are made, supported by witness (quotation) or evidence (reference) and then argued more fully. The second, allowed more with those not going on to further academic study, has sometimes also provided for a wider range of gaming — telling the story from the point of view of another character in the book (Tom Stoppard used that device in his **Rosencrantz and Guildenstern are Dead);** writing a poem back at the text (Auden did that with his poems on **The Tempest).** These link with such activities as keeping impressionistic diaries as the reading process goes on; drawing; sculpting; making film scripts; making audiotape versions; making drama; responding as the affective and cognitive drives suggest.

I have presented those in fairly extreme forms in order to raise a moral issue for us. The first of those devices is one often expected of our students in later academic life; it helps develop certain forms of intellectual discipline and promotes unambiguous presentation. It can also be assessed against publicly stated criteria. The second recognizes the nature of response as process and tolerates the personal, the exploratory, the unresolved. Its advocates concede low reliability but argue for high validity on the basis that literary response is to be seen in terms of unique event — that test and that person at that time making that dynamic relationship, whatever form it may take.

I see no easy resolution to the dilemma of these two modes, beyond employing both. I raise it simply to remind myself of it. Inquiry into the **nature** of response seems to me the priority for our talents and energies; we have much to learn there if the dilemma is to be debated and coped with in ways which value the complex event so neatly labelled with the phrase "reading fiction."

Seen on a Montreal church on the eve of this conference:
> The initial religious fact is the existence of other persons, individual and unique persons, with all their thoughts, hopes and fears, their motivations and needs.

Part Three

Oracy: Assessment of Speaking and Listening

When Manitoba teachers first saw that they were mandated to teach oracy, haunted as they were by the spectre of the Moral Majority and Renaissance International, they ran to their Oxford dictionaries to see if it was fitting and proper to teach this in the classroom.

So I would like to give you some definitions provided in our morning seminar: Joanne Bevis said that oracy raised all language from blasphemy to doxology; Joyce Matheson identified it as a shrine to be found somewhere in England; Mike Hayhoe described oracy as a wider view of languagecy; and John Dixon told us that oracy was civilization dawning.

Thus began the later plenary session report of discussion in the "Oracy" seminar. As with the Reading and Literature seminar, the formal offerings were few, perhaps reflecting the relatively little formal attention within the English teaching profession that to date has been given to the assessment of listening and speaking.

In his earlier paper, concerning the work of Assessment of Performance Unit, Michael Hayhoe commented on hopeful beginnings. I include here his formal paper examining more extensively the work and approach the APU has undertaken in oracy and the issues from this standpoint, as well as his less formal presentation within the seminar, "Assessing Oracy." Among a number of difficult technical problems in large-scale assessment of oral language, that of **intrusion** and consequent inauthenticity of the activity under assessment is perhaps the most serious. One encounters the problem in varying degrees in other assessment, though there are imaginative, if not widespread, tactics that may be employed to compensate partly for the intrusion. In both Hayhoe papers some excellent task/occasion suggestions are made and there are hints of how assessment might proceed. This, however, is certainly only the beginning of the matter.

One hopes that strategies developed at this level for large-scale assessment will provide the classroom teachers with better clues for oral language assessment, which in most settings amounts to little more than a "classroom participation" score enhanced perhaps by marks for public speaking or debating, both highly artificial activities (certainly not "everyday use of language"). John Dixon's "Four Ages of Assessing Spoken English" provides a light-hearted visit to the scene, and his paper also sets out the questions that should serve as departure points in undertaking oral language assessment.

So, as with Reading and Literature, the Oracy seminar was productive in setting out a number of the central issues. Additionally, here, the papers sketched a number of strategies that may be pursued. A beginning, at least.

The Assessment of Oracy

A Report with Observations on the Work of the Language Monitoring Team of the Assessment of Performance Unit in the United Kingdom

Michael J. Hayhoe
University of East Anglia

General Background

The initial work of the APU Language Monitoring Team was to develop assessment devices applicable to reading and writing, looking at performance at 11 and 15. While work on oracy was seen as important, there was some insecurity about it, including the issues of whether assessment devices could avoid artificiality and testing devices could avoid distorting the event being assessed.

Background to the Assessment of Oracy

Discussions ran from 1976 to 1978 about extending the team's work to include oracy. The issues which were debated have not been made fully public but are known to have included:

a) dissatisfaction with oral examinations at sixteen (the end of compulsory education), with many of the activities used to assess language performance being seen as artificial and presenting an odd view of oracy to the pupil, and with assessment criteria and their application being seen as often of poor quality;

b) recognition that the promotion of oral skills was not a major curricular feature in some schools. This raised the issue of whether the team should limit itself to monitoring what schools were actually doing, so providing a "true" picture of the state of education or whether it had a right to affect the curriculum through promoting assessment in this area;

c) concern over the asymmetrical nature of much testing. The team had nailed its colours to the mast much earlier by declaring that it saw language as a collaborative activity in which participants "made shared meaning;"

d) doubt about whether it is possible to monitor standards of oracy over time.

The team decided to start its work from scratch.[2] Details of its studies and visits, consultations and in-house development are not known. Because of staffing constraints, piloting did not begin until 1981, with the first testing taking place in 1982, in the form of a national survey at 11.

The Premises of Testing

General

a. Testing should look at pupils of 11 and 15, initially.
b. Testing should be carried out by means of "light sampling."
c. Testing should be responsive to the curriculum and avoid curricular backwash."
d. Testing should simulate features of the "real life" situation by creating a context which demands a "purposeful" use of language for an identifiable audience. "Language is a cooperative process."

Specific to Oracy

a. Oral performance involves listening and speaking, seen as aspects of communication.
b. Aspects of oral activities should not be explored as isolates. Nor should oral and reading/writing activities be separated.
c. Oracy is a cross-curricular activity and should be explored as such.
d. APU assessment should be based on "good class practice," seen usually in terms of teacher's "planned intervention" in promoting "sustained and purposeful talk" which promotes the learning process.

The Context of Testing

a. The context must reduce "communicative stress" to the minimum.
b. The setting should that of the children's school.
c. The child's teacher should be participant (usually an initiator and communicator of items) and intuitive (but guided) assessor.
d. In pair work, the main device used so far, "Jane" is chosen by computer from the reading sample of pupils, but "Jane" chooses her own partner.
e. Some pair work is now leading to group work. The team is confident that it can assess performance within this.

Tasks

List of Task Types

- Interpreting instructions for constructing a model (original)
- Interpreting instructions on how to play a board game and relaying these to other pupils for them to play the game.
- Interpreting an account of process and explaining the process to other pupils with the aid of a set of drawings (web weaving?)
- Interpreting an autobiographical account and going on to give an autobiographical account.
- Interpreting and re-telling a story to a group.
- Describing a set of pictures and creating a narrative on that basis. In discussion, re-sequencing the pictures to explore other narrative possibilities.
- Describing the work undertaken by someone in a particular occupation and stating a point of view concerned with it — work involving role play.
- Describing an experiment to another pupil, after observing how it is conducted, so that the second pupil can carry it out. The 2 pupils then collaborate in suggesting why it provided the results that it did.

- Interpreting as individuals information on a plant, each by studying the text and pictures provided. "Jane" tells "Jim" about her plant and about the pros and cons of trying to grow it as a crop. "Jim" tells "Jane" about his. They are then given details of an island and asked to discuss which plant would do best there. One of the pupils is asked to make a written account of the results of the discussions; the other, an oral one.
- The team is developing tasks involving "structured group discussion," carried out by supervised and unsupervised groups in a range of contexts. Details of these have not yet been made public.

Assessment

Assessment goes through a series of three stages.

1. The teacher-assessor makes a "controlled impression" assessment during the assessment event, arriving at a judgment on the relative performance of each pupil, based on a seven point scale.

2. The assessment event is an audio-tape and impression marked by a panel of teacher-assessors, using the same seven point scale.

These assessments are used for work commissioned by the APU on comparing the performance of groups of pupils chosen because of particular background variables. These have not been made public, but in the case of speakers of English as a first or second language, such school variables as single sex and mixed schools, pupil-teacher ratios, proportion of free school meals taken, and regional location are used.

3. A sample of audiotapes is chosen at random and assessed by means of reference to a range of specific criteria.

The assessment criteria have not been published but it looks as if they bear witness to the team's decision to start from scratch. In an unpublished paper, the Director, Dr. Tom Gorman wrote:

The criteria are derived from an analysis of a large number of recordings of pupils performing the tasks in question. We have worked backwards, as it were, from the impression marks awarded, selecting tapes exemplifying 'good, bad and indifferent' scores to work out what were the specific qualities of the tapes that elicited the impression marks assigned.[3]

Details of the discussion process by means of which these criteria were arrived at are not known. Four clusters of criteria are used:

1. Propositional Content
2. Sequential Structure
3. Lexico-Grammatical Features
4. Performance Features (Orientation to Listener included)

The first three are seen as applying to all tasks — but with particular subordinate criteria being appropriate to the activity being assessed. In the paper already mentioned, Dr. Gorman comments on Sequential Structure:

> The use of this category reflected the notion that speech events characteristically display a rhetorical or thematic structure, such that certain elements or episodes are expected to occur, and in a sequential order. But the actual components of the structure of particular speech events will vary: the structure of a narrative being different from that of an account of a process, for example.[4]

Category 4 acknowledges performance features which assessors have found do affect their judgments, such as hesitation phenomena, the extent of backtracking and self-correction and the matter of audibility and tempo.

Assessment and Significance

APU has tended to rely on the Rasch model, with its assumption of two features: one the so-called "difficulty" of an item and the other the "ability" of the person being tested. "Difficulty" assumes that an item's difficulty is unchanging. It assumes that, whatever child takes a test, the items will still be in the same sequence of difficulty. The model also assumes an individual's response is determined by one single ability trait — an odd idea, given pupils' varying experiences, personalities, educational and cultural backgrounds. It is not known how far (if at all) Rasch remains a significant research tool among the "statistical theologians." The Language Monitoring Team is provided with its own statistician and is looking at the statistical implications of such techniques as giving marks to pairs of pupils on components of tasks in which each pupil's performance is necessarily affected by that of his or her partner, for example when discussing the plant crop simulation. The team has not yet published its methods here but seems confident that they "work." In fact, they find their more serious constraint is that of identifying voices on group audiotapes. Data from the analytic marking are exploited to identify the demand features of the various tasks, thus following the practice of the team in its analytic marking of writing tasks.

Comment

1. The project has tried, as far as possible, to carry out its aim of keeping a low profile in the assessment by using a known site and adult (who behaves, a least partly, in an expected role); by providing for the presence of at least one chosen peer, by trying to develop genuinely interesting tasks.

2. As with its work in reading and writing, the team has been interested in modifying and extending its assessment techniques in the light of experience: the more recent work on unsupervised groups may be an example.

3. The grading techniques have worked from the intuitive and impressionistic, developing sets of criteria deemed to be purpose and audience appropriate.

4. The team has stuck to its intention of seeing language as a co-operative and communicative act, best assessed by activities which echo the actuality of "best" classroom practice and at least some of the uses of language in the "normal" world.

Issues

1. How far do such "simulars" encompass the range of oral language a child (as opposed to a pupil) uses at 11?

2. Most of the tasks described so far have an agenda built into them. How far is this agenda due to the task, how far due to the setter of the task? How is a pupil's own agenda-making assessed?

3. Many of the tasks described so far are assigned by the teacher-assessor to instruct or explain to the other. How far is such assigned asymmetry taken into account when evaluating performance?

4. In the case of writing and reading, devices other than tests are used — both are exploring attitudes towards themselves; pupils are invited to send in examples of their best writing as well as their APU assessment work. What devices might assist the team's inquiry into oral performance?

5. To what extent is audiotape analysis adequate at stages 2 and 3?

6. What are the details of the 1-7 impression scale; the analytic criteria; the statistical methods being used; the training methods used to develop the teacher-assessors?

7. It becomes increasingly clear that the "isness" stance of the early APU shows signs of becoming a "couldbeness" stance, if not an "oughtness" one, in due course. The team's director has spoken of the identification of specific features of variations in oral performance and has said that such a development has "pedagogical implications." Peter Gannon, of Her Majesty's Inspectorate, has written that "once it is possible to publish the assessment framework in full, it is, to my mind, likely that it will be of considerable help to teachers."[5] The issue here is one of how teachers will be informed; of how they will be supported in their professional development and debate over the APU findings; of how far they will be supported by society, should they wish to implement some of the teaching-learning and assessment procedures this work espouses. At the moment, APU works through light sampling of anonymised schools and pupils. It thus has much to commend it as an illuminative and issue-raising device, once its findings and premises are made open.

Notes

1. For the fullest account **so far** of the general workings of the APU, see Gipps C. and Goldstein H. (1983), **Monitoring Children: An Evaluation of the Assessment of Performance Unit,** London: Heinemann Education Books.

2. A definition of the team's focus supplied by Peter Gannon, HMI, in "Assessing the Spoken Word" in **APU Newsletter 3,** Spring 1983.

3. From paper by Dr. Tom Gorman, director of the APU's language team — "The Scope of the Exercise." My thanks to him for this and for discussions with him and his colleagues.

4. Ibid.

5. Op. cit.

Assessing Oracy

M.J. Hayhoe
University of East Anglia

There is an ambivalence about assessing oracy. One argument is that oral performance needs to be assessed, if only to signal to the wider world that oral skills are **the** basic language skills. Counter arguments reveal anxiety about the subjectivity of assessment and about the issue of "spying," that so many forms of talk involve relationships and trust, not judgmental surveillance.

Perhaps much learning through writing and reading does go on in school, more than goes on outside it — but the same may not apply in the case of oracy. How far can in-school assessment mirror beyond-school uses of talking and listening? Much talking and listening are contributed in order to be valued rather than evaluated, as they phase into and out of other activities — even into and out of silence. How is such "real" oracy to be assessed?

Perhaps the talking and listening which go on beyond the school cannot be assessed, but what about where it "really" happens inside? I think of a class of fourteen year olds spending half a term of English work on the theme *Autumn*, setting up by class and group discussion their own agenda of activities; of their going out to interview people of all ages and pursuits in their rural town about how the season still affected their lives; of the various forms of presentation that they devised and developed, some oral, some pictorial, some written. I recall ten year olds taping the old people in their village, asking them about their childhoods; fourteen year olds talking with old people and writing their biographies for them over a term, for them to keep or to present to the town archives. I remember fourteen year olds watching infants in a playground and discussing how they played; talking with the children about what they would like to play with and on; devising and making new equipment in metalwork and testing it with the infant clients. You and I could make an endless list of contexts, many more spectacular than these and many more or less obvious in which real talk has taken place, briefly or over a great deal of time. Not to assess it is to exclude it. How to assess it without adversely affecting it?

In fact, many schools find daily occasions for "real" talk. They may also provide "simulars:" tasks and activities which in some way may mirror beyond-school situations and which promote the aims of the Bullock Report to promote **focused** talk and act as "exercises in extension." These can range from socio-drama to simulations and problem-solving tasks — working out an advertising campaign for everyone in town on the day that traffic has to start driving on the other side of the road; making decisions as school children, shopkeepers, bus company managers, property developers about the siting of an airport in the neighbourhood, and so on. These can go alongside the more usual forms, such as debates and lecturettes.

So far, assessment of oracy has been limited in the United Kingdom. Its main place comes in examinations at 16 + , signalling the end of compulsory education, and there it is to be found most usually in the Certificate of Secondary Education syllabus, an award for students not in the top 20% ability range. For many of the C.S.E. boards, performance in spoken English is assessed half by course assessment over the preceding four or five terms and half by end of course "test." As always, the advocates of this practice see the course work providing opportunity for high validity; the opponents chances for low reliability. Moves are afoot for a new examination at 16 + which will cater for the top 60% of the school population, using such devices as group discussion, individual conversations, reading tests, prepared talks and aural comprehensions. Clearly there is much to be done if some rather weary practices are not to be dusted and re-displayed under a new label. Some see possibilities for a wider range of techniques and for clearer criteria coming from the work of the Assessment of Performance Unit.

Four Ages of Assessing Spoken English

John Dixon

Today I must be brief. But I am old enough as a teacher to have seen four ages in the assessment of spoken English, starting with the Old Stone Age and approaching — as I come towards the end of my allotted span — quite near to Civilization. Let me tell you a story.

In the Old Stone Age when I was a boy and a beginning teacher, we used what I call the "Elocution" model. Pupils read aloud in a clear voice, or gave lecturettes, I remember — and I had difficulties in my first year class in 1951 when the youngest member of the British Interplanetary Society exceeded his two minutes. You weren't supposed to get carried away like that. The criteria were concerned with other things: was the pronunciation clear, the volume adequate, the pace neither too quick nor too ponderous, the intonation not monotonous but lively, and was the English "correct" — with not too much of a regional accent, please. Marks were given out of 5 or 10, and, by way of variation, the class themselves were sometimes allowed to vote on the appropriate mark to give.

Somewhere around 1960, the first tape recorders arrived in my school (weighing around 30 lbs.) and a New (Stone) Age dawned. Among other things we discovered "the interview:" the notion was that an intelligent examiner should do the best possible by questions and comments to elicit fluent, coherent and interesting speech from a student interviewee. As soon as my department took this seriously we discovered to our surprise — and delight — that almost the whole group of school leavers were really very enjoyable people to interview. It caused a certain amount of heart-searching: why hadn't we known before? Perhaps our students had more to say for themselves than we'd imagined. Assessing "oracy" (the new name) became just a little problematic; but for the moment interviewing was added to reading and lecturettes.

Then serious tape recording experiments began. In 1964 Nancy Martin was running a "Talk & Talkers" group with London teachers. We listened with great excitement to their tapes of four or five students discussing a poem on their own — without the teacher! Then, with horror, we listened to ourselves "discussing" the same poem with a class: now we knew why we'd underestimated pupils' oral capabilities — we'd dammed them up. So a Bronze Age began, when we tried hard to think of ways to get small groups talking, and possibly "reporting back" in a plenary session to the class. We were into a model of Dialogue and Communication. But it was harder to think of suitable assessment methods. A group discussion changes when the teacher listens — or even when the tape recorder does. We tried to think of a Communication model for more public kinds of assessment, and ended up with things like this: a student gives a prepared talk to a small peer group, with the assessor listening in; the group acts as audience, raising intelligent questions and considering the answers; and the speaker may take part in the follow-up discussion (helped by a chairperson he or she has chosen). So you end up being assessed in several roles, as Speaker, Chair, Questioner, Responder to Questions, and Group Discussant. You get hints of this new age in **Language, the Learner, and the School** by Barnes, Britton & Rosen (1969).

At this point the more radical among us began to reject "formal" asessment of speech and to opt for "sampling" assessment during normal course work. This sounded like a Millennium, but the question remained, what exactly were the students supposed to be learning to do — what counted towards competence in Oral Communication? We're still trying to make the answers (and our practice) more precise, detailed and theoretically sound.

I can say this much:

1. Looking at the individual you need to clarify:

a) What range of purposes the student is learning (and choosing to learn) to speak for.
(Reciting and reading aloud can be added as a minor element.)
b) What range of audiences the student is learning to speak to, for various purposes.
c) What visual aids and other secondary modes of communication the student is learning to use alongside speech.

2. Looking at groups of students, you need to clarify:

a) What forms of dialogue (and roles) they are learning to good effect, including interview explanatory discussion, planning and decision-making, and various kinds of dramatic interaction.
b) What range of purposes for using language are incorporated in these various forms of dialogue.

At present, this kind of thinking results in a rough check-list. This is not really difficult to produce for individual monologue, because the theoretical work on writing is quite a help; with dialogue, however, a theoretical model isn't readily available, and what there is seems rather complex. Checklists tend to remain pretty crude. But then, only sophisticated teaching methods allow students during their courses a regular chance to make group decisions, or to make joint plans, or to interview other people. A Civilised age in Oral Assessment awaits more civilised ways of learning and teaching.

Still, here and there efforts **are** being made. And, as they occur, some new assessment heresies are emerging. For instance, if you get a complex set of judgments, such as the check-list promotes, why express them as a grade — which conceals most of the real information — rather than some form of profile? And since much of social life depends on group effort and achievement, shouldn't we sometimes be assessing a group rather than the individual? There are even teachers of 17 to 18 year-olds who discuss with groups how to avoid "blocking" each other and how to promote effective group discussion — and realise what they are doing. It sounds to me at times as if Civilisation is quite close.

Part Four

Standardized Tests and Alternatives

The use of commercial standardized tests is widespread in the United States and Canada, and their frequent mindless use, at least in Canada, for purposes they were never designed to serve has become an extremely serious problem for the English teaching profession - a problem more serious than many teachers appear to recognize. It was for this reason that the subject was chosen as a seminar topic in Montreal.

For Australia and the United Kingdom, the problem does not seem so severe, though the Bullock Report, **A Language For Life,** in Chapter Two "Standards of Reading," uses evidence from the dated Watts-Vernon test as support for introducing more effective alternatives to British schools.

Within the seminar John Hutchins reported that in Australia education is fundamentally a state matter. There is no national standardized testing program and little state-wide testing, though on occasion there is cooperation among states in surveys of "basic skills." While there is sporadic political pressure for "accountability" surveys, very little pressure comes from teachers for such testing. On one occasion teachers in Western Australia simply refused to participate in a testing program! Whether, Hutchins noted, in today's climate that refusal would be accepted is another question. On the other hand, there has been a recent trend to more diagnostic testing. The usual problems have emerged concerning a match between authentic performance and the artificiality of test situations, and, to date, he reported, no test has been found that leads directly to improved instruction.

There was no American resource person at this seminar, so we have no report of the effect many excellent studies (e.g. Kenneth Goodman, Roger Farr, Richard Venezky) of the shortcomings of standardized tests of reading have had there, nor of the impact of the 1975 NCTE Task Force Report on measurement and evaluation, **Common Sense and Testing in English.** Certainly many resources are available as means of protection against bad testing and misuse of scores, though if these resources are brought to bear as ineffectively in the United States as they are in Canada, the problem has certainly not disappeared.

The Standardized Tests and Alternatives seminar was, unlike the other seminars, designed to address chiefly **Canadian** concerns. My own presentation was in the form of a report, with commentary, on the CCTE survey, conducted through the CCTE newsletter in the fall of 1982, of the use of standardized tests in English and the Language Arts. Dr. R. Wilson of Queen's University contrasted the standardized test with the increasingly popular alternative, criterion-referenced testing, noting some of the pitfalls of the latter. His presentation was chiefly intended to challenge the claim of superiority of criterion-referenced tests over traditional norm-referenced tests. The claim would lead people "to assume that response to an item is a clearer vision of the truth." In his introduction, he expressed his dismay over the current tendency by distributors of norm-referenced tests to market them as serviceable also as criterion-referenced tests. This misrepresents both the basis of test design and item selection and the real strength of the norm-referenced test as a useful measure of general skills development. "The attempt to match such tests to specific bits and pieces of curriculum is misplaced effort." Mr. W. Allan from Nelson's (a major test distributor in Canada) spoke briefly concerning cautions and advice in the use of standardized tests. Preceding his presentation he alluded to his more formal remarks at the invitational session on the preceding day when he outlined current challenges and opportunities for the testing industry. Because technological changes, of which the English profession is largely unaware, are making an impact there, I have included here his remarks from both days.

Although what is presented here is only the gist of their remarks, as reconstructed from notes, both the publisher's and the statistician's perspective need to be represented if we are to begin to cope at all with measurement issues.

My own concerns will be evident from my presentation, but I should like to re-state boldly two of those:

1. It is essential, for the sake of our students, that those who **use** commercial tests understand fully their limits of measure and report those limitations properly in any use made of such scores to judge or classify students.

2. It is not enough to deplore or pretend to ignore indifferent or poor tests. Teachers and consultants must take responsible roles in ascertaining the **validity** of any tests proposed and in decisions concerning use and limits of use.

At present in Canada commercial tests are widely used, with, in most settings, no evidence whatever of such scrutiny. While teachers are becoming increasingly alert to and concerned about large-scale assessment undertakings at a provincial level, this professional concern does not appear to extend to the encroachment of this other type of external measurement upon the classroom.

Trends in Educational Measurement: A Publisher's perspective

Bill Allan
Nelson Publishers

Measurement theory employed in commercial test development has changed very little so far in this century, and there have been misuses of standardized test results. However, today's educator is more discriminating, and interest is growing in criterion-referenced testing as well, with the recognition that the standardized test was never designed to measure all types of educational outcomes. The interest in criterion-referenced tests has extended to development at the local level of curriculum-specific instruments.

There are three trends in technical development which offer considerable promise:

  (i)   Statistical refinement
  (ii) Advances in machine scoring
  (iii) The computer and storage

This last has brought about development (e.g. at the Educational Research Institute of British Columbia) of item banking. Here the potential of the computer in storing, retrieving, and manipulating test data is virtually unlimited. And new testing frameworks are now possible, one of particular interest being **adaptive** testing, which permits prompt adjustment of a test item sequence to the individual student's ability and avoids waste in testing time over items too easy or too difficult.

The microcomputer, too, provides exciting potential, though at present the diversity of hardware in schools is a problem.

Advances in machine scoring through scanning have vastly improved turn-around time, and scoring options have become more diverse and sophisticated. Local scoring services, commercial and non-commercial, and desk-top scanners are with us, too. These developments in scoring service are perceived by commercial publishers as a threat, and publishers are tending to hold back from new enterprises as a result.

From the standpoint of traditional test theory, statistical refinements in item response theory, matrix sampling, and the emergence of a statistical model (contrasted with the normal curve) for criterion-referenced testing are of great interest.

New sampling techniques, especially matrix sampling, have resulted in effective evaluation along with a corresponding saving in both time and resources.

The traditional variance model by definition is inapplicable to criterion-reference tests (mean and deviation scores versus per cent achieving an objective). A growing body of statistics is being developed to describe this measure.

Specific Areas of Current Investigation in English:

1. Community College and University entrance examinations have become a target of considerable interest in parts of Canada with concern for sound diagnosis of post-admission needs of post-secondary candidates.

2. The assessment of communication skills, especially the assessment of writing, requires some reasonably objective method of measurement, and the areas of speaking and listening are now coming under attention.

3. Finally, with respect to "comprehension" and the processes involved in reading, research is now challenging the construct validity of current tests.

All of these are areas deserving activity by test publishers, but they are difficult areas and publishers are diffident about large investment in them at this time.

The Use of Standardized Tests

Bill Allan
Nelson Publishers

1. Why Standardized Tests?

They provide an additional perspective to complement teachers' information at the classroom level. The normative data permits comparison of achievement levels. And the instruments may be of better **quality** than similar instruments developed employing only local resources.

2. How to Choose a Standardized Test:

Because content validity is essential for an achievement test, an item by item inspection of a test is necessary to establish whether a suitable match exists between the test and local curriculum.

No standardized test, no matter how carefully planned and constructed, can ever be equally well suited for use in all schools; there are local differences in curricular objectives, grade placement, and instructional emphasis, as well as differences in the nature and characteristics of the student population. These should be taken into account in evaluating the validity of a test for local use.

3. Cautions in Interpreting Standardized Tests:

A norm is only a description of average achievement and should not be considered as a standard or as an indication of what constitutes "satisfactory" achievement.

A test score is simply one more tool a teacher has available to help evaluate a student; it must be used in conjunction with all other information a teacher has.

Standardized test results may be used as a partial basis for evaluating the effectiveness of instruction. Batteries such as **The Canadian Tests of Basic Skills*** are concerned only with certain basic skills and only those areas which are particularly amenable to objective measurement. Other less tangible but equally important outcomes should not be neglected.

*Editor's note: **The Canadian Tests of Basic Skills** battery is a Canadian adaptation of the **Iowa Tests of Basic Skills** developed in the United States.

Standardized and Criterion-Referenced Tests

Bob Wilson
Queen's University

The most frequently mentioned alternative to standardized tests is the criterion-referenced tests. In most important ways, such tests promise to do more damage to the teaching-learning environment than norm-referenced tests ever did.

The flaws in criterion-referenced tests:

1. They neglect to indicate that a response to an item allows us to infer learning; we do not measure learning directly. While verisimilitude may often be desirable, it is by no means sufficient. The responses are still indicators, not the learning itself.

2. They assume that the ability to perform Task A is in some important way independent of the ability to perform Task B. Factor analytic studies demonstrate fairly conclusively that some general abilities underlie performance on a wide variety of tasks and subject areas, especially in the elementary grades.

3. They aid in the simplistic notion that a curriculum is the sum of many discrete bits. The generalizability of knowledge in an important validation technique, and one that criterion-referenced tests, by definition, ignore.

4. They ignore measurement error. As in other tests purporting to measure "the thing itself," any mistake is assumed to be the learner's — a ludicrous claim for any measurement instrument. (By contrast the standardized testing industry acknowledges and specifies error of measurement.)

Good standardized tests can be used for just the kind of validation that criterion-referenced tests ignore. They would have to be independent of the specific objectives in any given curriculum. They need to have construct validity - the constructs being those generic abilities that seem to underlie success in living a healthy, democratic, purposeful life.

The usual criticism of a standardized achievement test, that it does not measure the specific objectives of a given curriculum, does not hold up. Reverse the question: If a child has been to school for X years, should he or she be able to answer an item like this? The test then becomes what it should be: a tool for evaluating **curriculum.**

The Use and Abuse of Standardized Tests

Peter Evans
Ontario Institute for Studies in Education

This paper is my report on the CCTE survey of testing practices in Canada undertaken through the CCTE Newsletter, Fall 1982. Beyond that, I wish to issue a few challenges and attempt to raise some questions for discussion. I hope to advance the following goals:

- that teachers of English more frequently play a major role in test selection and decisions concerning use;

- that testing be undertaken only for clear and valid purposes, especially the purpose of improving the English program;

- that test data not be used beyond the limits of precision which characterize the particular test or be extrapolated into judgements about student performance beyond what the test is designed to measure;

- that professional teachers begin to demand that the "industry" build tests that are truly valid, reflecting a reasonable range of important objectives in much more imaginative ways than at present and reflecting what we know, for example, about language and reading development.

I could follow at once with a sermon on any of the above that would last long and probably get us no further along. You may properly conclude that I believe very strongly that it is at present the case in most school systems that teachers of English and Language Arts have little to say about test selection and little understanding of the characteristics of standardized tests that are being employed. There is, with ignorance, a kind of reverence for scores, both by teachers and administrators, a faith, I would say, that makes the Flat Earth Society, by comparison, a credible organization.

You might also conclude that I am angry with the testing industry itself, but I am not. I once was, and before that I was true believer: if a test was in print, if it was long enough, if it had a prestigious title, and if it provided percentile or grade equivalent scores, which I then thought I understood, it had to be good. Well, I lost my faith some years ago and, quite naturally, began taking my anger out on the testing industry.

And there are some things seriously wrong there, right enough. I will detour later into one of those wrongs which remains serious. But my anger or rather, frustration, has shifted to ourselves: to the gullibility of the English profession and, it should be added, to educational researchers in English who quite blithely and, perhaps (to give them the benefit of the doubt, at least with respect to their knowledge base), cynically prop up their conclusions in one study after another with reference to standardized test data.

I cannot really blame a testing industry that simply continues, perhaps with some refinements as the universe unfolds, to give people what they are willing to buy. The industry has not been challenged to go back to fundamentals. In some of my own test development work, I share some of that guilt, if guilt it is, of giving people what they wanted or claimed to want. It is high time, however, that we began telling the testing industry what we **do** want, what we are prepared to accept, and what we are no longer prepared to tolerate. That will produce a rather immediate effect, I assure you.

I invited Bill Allan of Nelson Publishers to the 1983 conference because he is prepared to listen. If we want more of the same, I am sure we'll get it; if we challenge the industry for something better, I think it reasonable to expect that we'll get that - if we press hard enough.

The CCTE Survey

The CCTE Fall 1982 **Newsletter** contained a survey form which all CCTE members associated with elementary and secondary education were asked to fill in and return before Christmas. The survey was an inquiry into the present use of standardized tests or locally developed alternatives in schools.

The survey was deliberately limited in its purposes. We wanted at that stage, without loading the questions or building in editorials, to discover just what in general was going on. I did not ask any questions related, for example, to validity of the sort I have mentioned in the report. Of course, I would like to, and am fairly certain of the answers. I hope each of you will ask questions exactly of that order, test by test, item by item. The first concern raised in the report is the purpose of testing. We wanted to investigate, in as neutral a way as possible, the extensiveness of use of standardized and other tests, the tests that predominate, and the kinds of uses made of the results.

There were 69 responses, quite unevenly distributed by province: for example, 25 from Saskatchewan (several from one system) and only 16 from Ontario. However, responses from a number of coordinators or superintendents on behalf of systems gave some practical enlargement of the survey, notably in British Columbia and Ontario. I know that if I followed up formally with coordinators and superintendents in many systems that I am familiar with in Ontario, I would obtain evidence of even greater "routine" use of commercial tests on a compulsory system-wide or school-wide basis than the survey documented, and, were I to press them further, the admission that the data are **not** effectively used (and for data from some appalling tests I am just as happy this is so) to evaluate or modify program. I don't have to go further than the schools my own children attend to discover in universal use the particularly ancient (1938) and appalling **Monroe-Sherman Test,** a test so bad it doesn't even merit a review in the **Mental Measurements Yearbook.** What would you turn up if **you** looked?

Evidence of **local** initiative in test design was, as expected, depressing.

Few schools or systems refer to locally built instruments other than regular school examinations. In B.C. there was evidence of writing assessment conducted within systems, and several systems in Ontario also conducted on a regular basis some form of writing assessment across the system. Cloze procedures for assessing reading were a feature in one large Ontario system; others in Ontario made use, usually on an optional basis, of instruments developed in the Ontario Assessment Instrument Pool for English in the Intermediate (Grades 7-10) Division. Another large system in Ontario had recently developed and put in use its own tests of reading and writing mechanics, and another had developed a reading skills inventory. Edmonton reported tests of spelling developed for some elementary grades. On the whole, however, there appeared to be little initiative in local development of assessment instruments to match program.

Response concerning tests available for **optional** use by teachers was rather confusing. The most frequently mentioned were (elementary) the **Gates-MacGinitie Reading** series, the **Canadian Tests of Basic Skills,** the **Metropolitan** and **Stanford Tests;** and (secondary) **Gates-MacGinitie (F),** the **Nelson-Denny Reading Test** and the **Stanford Diagnostic Reading Test.**

The question about system-wide testing elicited responses from approximately 37 systems; for 23 of these systems system-wide testing with commercial standardized tests was conducted. In some instances we found combined provincial/system with data from provincial testing required by the system, and additional system-only tests. System-wide testing received generally more emphasis at elementary than at secondary.

As to school-wide achievement, a number of responses were from superintendents or consultants, some of whom noted that school-wide assessment occurred in some of their schools and not in others. One admitted to being unsure of the situation. Additionally, system-wide testing involved the school. Hence it is difficult from our responses to obtain an accurate picture of the prevalence of compulsory school-based use (as distinct from system-wide).

Where we did have clear response by schools, nine schools note system only, seven schools note school only, fourteen schools note both.

The tests employed most frequently by far were the **Canadian Tests of Basic Skills** (Nelson) and the **Gates-MacGinitie Reading Test** series, now also distributed by Nelson. The CTBS tests are normed for about Grades 3-9 and are employed across various combinations of these grades. Levels C, D, E, and F of the Gates-MacGinitie tests were used from Grades 4 into Secondary School. Frequently the publication date provided in the survey responses indicates that the most recent edition of the Gates-MacGinitie test was not yet in use. With some tests, the edition matters little; with Gates-MacGinitie, however, there have been major changes (in this writer's opinion, improvements) in the most recent edition.

Other commercial tests were mentioned much less frequently, though the recently published **Canadian Achievement Test** (McGraw Hill) was mentioned several times as were various editions of the **Stanford** Tests. One system employed the **OISE** (1977) **Reading and Language** tests which have Canadian norms.

One teacher from a school for native students noted that the Department of Indian Affairs and Northern Development **requires** CTBS data; the teacher expressed fear of cultural disadvantage, and this is certainly a matter deserving scrutiny.

Use of Student Scores

Several survey questions pertained to the recording and use made of individual student scores. Overwhelmingly scores are recorded either as percentiles or grade-equivalent scores, neither of which reflect the built-in error of measure. Stanines and percentile bands are each mentioned only twice.

Twenty-one schools' responses indicate that scores are retained for classroom use; 33 responses indicate that scores are attached to the student's permanent record or file. There are, of course, a number of instances of both. What is striking and puzzling is that even where sampling rather than every-pupil testing is indicated, quite often the score goes into the student's record nevertheless. Frankly, this makes little sense.

Teachers were asked whether standardized test scores were used for streaming/grouping, for promotion, both, or neither. Pertinent responses (by **school** only):

Streaming/Grouping ONLY	- 11
Promotion (as a factor) ONLY	- 4
Both S/G and Promotion	- 11
"Neither"	- 5 (Though 3 of these noted the form in which scores are recorded)
No column checked	- 7 (Though 5 noted the form in which scores are recorded.)

Additionally three of five coordinator/superintendent responses which addressed this question stated "both" for their respective systems' schools, and two put in question marks. One teacher (from a private school) noted that test results were included in admissions criteria.

When the question was posed in the survey, it was anticipated that very few would claim that standardized test scores would receive use in promotion decisions. However, school responses reveal the practice as quite extensive. The critical question, then, becomes HOW they are used? What degree of precision is assumed for score? One can imagine a promotion meeting where a student with an unusually high reading or language score but a class mark of 45 is given the nod; one can, unhappily, also imagine the decision concerning the student with an unusually low standardized test score and a class mark of 48.

Confusion in some of the responses (no claim of use, but precise information on method of recording scores) possibly reflects confusion concerning policy and practice within the school.

Leaving aside entirely the vital question of validity, of what these tests measure or purport to measure, the undue respect given test **scores** is a matter of grave concern.

Here I do have a bone to pick most seriously with the marketers of commercial tests. This important information, the limits on the precision of measure, is usually buried in the technical manual, and not provided or else not adequately explained in the administrator's manual from which teachers derive grade equivalent or percentile scores from raw scores. Indeed in all the packaging hype teachers are led entirely away from this consideration. I recall in the administrator's manual of a prestigious test a note of caution on one page recommending against grade equivalent scores, and the provision on the following page of the full table of them.

Only ETS of any marketers I know shows full integrity in not giving G.E. scores and further (at least on the Cooperative English Test student sheet) dictates reporting performance by percentile **band** and measure of growth by non-overlapping bands, precisely to take into account the error of measurement. And, even then, the caution is "reasonable certainty."

Teachers and administrators don't know that, and so a percentile score of, say, 40 which may translate into a G.E. score 1 1/2 grades below the student's place, leads rather immediately to a judgement which may, unfortunately, be shared with the student, parent, or promotion tribunal that the child is "a slow reader," "having reading difficulties," "reading below grade level" when in fact the student's true score, taking into account the standard error of measurement, may be at the 50th percentile or higher. For any observed score (the score obtained in a single administration), there are only 2 chances in 3 that the "true" score falls within the error of measurement which itself, especially in midrange scores, may cross 10 percentiles or more! To announce a rough approximation (even were the test wholly valid, wholly reliable, and properly comprehensive) as an exact measure is a most serious misrepresentation.

While the error of measurement does average out for **groups**, it creates an important ethical problem in interpreting individual scores. Individual scores, if there is some reason for reporting them, should always be reported in percentile bands, or preferably stanines.

It is also worth noting that many published norms are quite inappropriate for groups one may have under test. I always recommend that, if normative information is required, a system develop its own norms over a minimum three year period.

Use of General Performance Data

Surely the expense and general discomfort entailed in such widespread use of such tests should have some pay-off for program. Response on this point, however, was not very encouraging. Teachers were asked whether data were used for program review (school, system, or, where relevant, province) or for some other purpose (to be stated), whether much use was ever made of the data, or whether they had any idea of what uses were made. The following is a summary from the 36 pertinent responses:

Of 36 responding, 27 maintained (though several of these only cautiously) that performance data were used at the school level in program review and 21 that they were similarly used at the system level. Of 18 from schools in provinces with provincial assessment, 10 believed that provincial data were used for program assessment and review. The other 8 expressed doubt that much use is ever made of the data or simply had no idea.

Of the 36 responding, 10 admitted to being quite unclear what uses, if any, were made of the data. These 10 include 5 of those noted above who claimed either school or system use in program review. 11 expressed themselves as fairly

58

certain that little or no use was actually made: i.e. that collecting performance information makes no difference. (There is considerable overlap of the "Really don't know" and "Don't think much or any" groups.)

Likely the foregoing summary reflects a picture more optimistic than the actual case. While 27 of 36 respondents believe some program-related use is made of the test results, I think many of them are responding in faith that surely someone somewhere is doing something.

Or what is done may be of this order:

I was involved some years ago on a curriculum development project in English, and had the good fortune to find a school staff willing to involve kids in a wide range of language activities — and more and varied writing. Things were going swimmingly. I visited the school some time later to catch up on what the kids were doing, and was sheepishly informed by the vice-principal that, well, in the CTBS testing a few weeks before, punctuation scores for the school had come out a little low, and the superintendent had ordered up punctuation drills. Consequently, of course, our work had been abandoned. The principal was unavailable. That's program revision.

To return to the report, a good many respondents conceded that no use was made of data or, if any was, they weren't aware of it.

Summary

The following questions and challenges conclude this paper:

1. That two tests (**CTBS** and **Gates-MacGinitie**) predominate so heavily must give us pause, especially as we know that the basic design of both is American. In the language and reading sections "Canadianization" is minor.

2. That most schools and systems record scores as "Grade Equivalent" and/or Percentiles (against the advice of trained psychometrists and such a prestigious firm as the Educational Testing Service at Princeton) suggests a faith in the precision of scores not sustained by the tests' own technical manuals.

3. The frequent use of standardized test scores in promotion decisions, taken with No. 2, is cause for real concern. How these scores are used is an important question.

4. That many teachers register doubts concerning the value for program or otherwise of annual or, at least frequent, large collections of data is a matter to consider. Many, on reflection, simply have no idea whether or how such data are used; others are quite cynical about both use and potential usefulness. Some teachers and coordinators are uncertain, even within their own school or system, about what is happening. It is clearly time, in all settings, to reflect upon what is being done and why, involving the teachers in that reflection.

5. Simply the many inconsistencies of use and apparent lack of a clear policy within a school or system suggest that schools at least should review carefully present practices. Some may be excellent, others redundant or wasteful, others misapplied.

Meantime, teachers of English and Language Arts surely have a responsibility to begin studying carefully tests in use, in hand, or under consideration, and to make their professional concern and curricular judgement felt wherever testing decisions are made. I add, with some trepidation, that I believe it is also teachers' professional responsibility to become sufficiently acquainted with the technical manual of any tests under consideration to know how the test was constructed, how (and where) normed, and the limits of precision of measure.

I commend for a start the excellent Task Force report on measurement and evaluation, **Common Sense and Testing in English** (1975) of the National Council of Teachers of English, and R.L. Venezky's **Testing in Reading: Assessment and Instructional Decision Making** (1974), also available from NCTE.

I believe CCTE, and the other national associations, have a responsibility as well — to provide detailed reviews of commercial tests related to English, and, through conferences and publications, to press important assessment issues upon the profession and the public.

Part Five

Writing Assessment

As noted at the outset, two seminars were specifically scheduled for writing assessment, one to report upon and discuss the large-scale context, and the other to focus more specifically on the student. However, because the seminar concerning post-secondary assessment also dealt exclusively with writing, all have been grouped as Part Five.

In the seminar concerned specifically with large-scale assessment there were reports of Canadian provincial activity (Bryan Roberts from New Brunswick, Stanley Straw for Manitoba, for example) and discussion of the International English Assessment approach (Alan Purves) and National Assessment of Educational Progress approach (Rexford Brown) with some heat, it was reported, generated over alternative scoring methods (holistic, primary trait, analytic) and types of counts such as T-Unit scores and error counts.

As the major Canadian reports can be obtained from the respective provincial Ministries or Departments of Education and extensive reports of the work of the National Assessment of Educational Progress are readily available, it would be futile to attempt digests of those projects here. The debate within that seminar around alternative scoring approaches, though undoubtedly of wide interest, is not retrievable except in frustrating fragments; the fundamental issue, I believe, goes back to what kinds of information, as discussed in the opening panel, are required by what audiences and who the legitimate audiences are.

The formal presentations from the writing assessment seminars have been arranged to move from the outside in: from large-scale assessment divorced from the classroom, to the classroom itself, and finally to specific students and specific compositions.

The first, by Garth Boomer, is his reflective reconstruction of his remarks vigorously opposing external assessment. From that paper the reader may infer the views Boomer expressed in his panel presentation. Andrew Wilkinson's paper, in which he reflects upon his experience in the Crediton project, describes a dilemma in the testing of writing and proposes a shift and expansion of categories for assessment. Ken Watson's paper (co-authored with Brian Johnston) is an expansion of the seminar presentation and shifts attention to the **classroom** and an alternative model for English assessment. Hayden Leaman's first paper, his seminar presentation, contrasts models of assessment at the level of school and classroom; his second, which he sent on following the seminar, completes the "zoom lens" sequence by focussing on the writing of individual students.

The Assessment of Writing

Garth Boomer
Former President
Australian Association for the Teaching of English

While I can appreciate some of the Canadian attempts to convert Ministry pressures into large-scale testing of writing which is of educational value to children and teachers, I must point out that with the best will in the world it is impossible to invent general **prompts** or **starting points** which will ensure that all those taking the tests **intend** to write. The imposition of a theme cuts across the basic condition for good writing: having something to say and wanting to say it. The work of Emig, Graves, Murray, Moffett and Britton, amongst many, progressively reinforces the significance of "authoring," the writer owning the task.

We know that when intention is low and cognitive engagement loose or muddled, syntax, structure, cohesion, and even spelling, fall apart. Results from wide scale tests may not therefore reflect actual competence. Thus by entering into a partnership with wide scale testing advocates, English teachers are required to do damage to the composing process, even if they devise tests which allow drafting, re-drafting and polishing time, because the essential factor of intent cannot be satisfactorily negotiated. In such a collusion with testers, we are as a profession holding up a flawed model of the composing process in writing and, by our patent demonstrations, condoning writing instruction which works on a stimulus-response model.

I note also that arguments are being advanced that training English teachers to be markers of writing produced under large-scale testing conditions is having clear "pay-offs" in terms of teachers' understanding of their own and others' criteria for assessing writing and raised awareness of implications for writing instruction to overcome perceived flaws. Wherever English teachers gather to look at children's writing and have the chance to talk about it, there will be a desirable raising of awareness and a better understanding of certain issues in writing, but I suggest that the **testing context** can skew attention towards **flaws** (both in the text and in the imagined teaching behind it) rather than **growth points.** This can lead too easily to a deficiency model of the writer and the writer's teachers.

I note, for instance, that the British Columbia project is suggesting, in reports to schools, areas where writing is falling down, and coming up with suggestions for appropriate writing **instruction** to remedy this. This focus on flaws and writing instruction as opposed to **growth points** and attention to the learner's engagement in the composing process seems to point English teaching in a direction *away* from what the research is telling us, towards **instruction in manipulation of language,** away from **tracking growth and providing appropriate new contexts to extend growth.**

This leads me to a further analysis of the possible effects of large-scale testing of writing on the teachers' sense of power and confidence. Where external testers produce results and reports and analysis (according to complex criteria) for teachers, and add to these observations on what needs to be done to get better writing, teachers are likely to see the locus of power, knowledge and judgement **outside** their own classrooms. This is likely to encourage deference, tentativeness and self-doubt in teachers, who will tend to focus on the examiners for guidance and a definition of the good, rather than on their own and their students' judgement. It is very difficult for examiners' reports not to drop into a register which directly or indirectly offers hints to those who desire to advance towards heaven. Now, if teachers feel deferential towards outside authorities, there will be a chain reaction passing on attitudes of "trying to please authority" to the students. The students will also find the locus of power and judgement outside themselves. Thus, ironically, we may cut children off from the personal power and intention that would make them good writers.

The Australian Association for the Teaching of English and State English Teachers Councils in Australia are for the above reasons, and others, opposed to the large-scale assessment of writing. Our energies are being concertedly directed towards the collaboration of teacher and student in developing productive ways of talking about writing, valuing it, and adopting new strategies for improvement. The work of Bill Hannan and Dr. Brian Johnston is directed towards the **empowerment** of students through vigorous evaluation procedures which are jointly owned and controlled by teacher and student.

With respect to large-scale work, we would ask that money be pumped into large-scale **research** commissioned by the profession and involving the profession in a quest to become more wise about abiding problems, as opposed to large-scale assessment which attempts to measure and quantify in ways which have little pedagogical yield and a wide range of negative effects on the ecology of the curriculum. In Australia, we would be supporting John Dixon's advice from the panel discussion that accountability for writing should be rigorously applied at the local school level by means of folios of children's work, displays, open forums, etc. The showing and sharing of texts composed by students will be at once a powerful means of showing present achievement and a focus for educative talk between teachers and the community about what constitutes good writing. By comparison, the meaning of cryptic measures and statistics is decidedly bankrupt.

Writing Assessment:
The Crediton Project

A.M. Wilkinson, Professor of Education
School of Education,
University of East Anglia

The usual criteria of judgment for writing in the classroom are too narrow. The effect of standardized examinations and graded tests is to narrow them still further because of a concern with what can be measured objectively; and since teachers reach towards the examinations and tests, such narrowed criteria become the classroom criteria. Of course such tests can be justified on political grounds, even on motivational grounds, for both teachers and students. It is only persons holding discredited beliefs about the functions of education in relation to the human spirit who find such justifications less than convincing.

Nevertheless it is unrealistic to ignore the fact of examinations and their function as a major instrument of curriculum control. We must work for examinations whose influence is benign, widening the criteria of judgment,· amongst other things. (Good) classroom practice should determine the examinations in the first place, not vice versa. Thus examinations including course work are more likely on the face of it to be on the way to this.

Assessment in the classroom should essentially be a teaching, not a measuring, device. We are constantly making assessments of where children are in order to help them to develop further. Our methods of assessment are related to our beliefs about our roles as teachers of language. If we are concerned to develop only the "skills" of writing, we choose (implicitly or explicitly) a marking scheme which rewards successful performance in these skills, and effectively makes other features of writing seem less important. The child becomes a spelling- or punctuation- or syntax-producing machine. But if we believe that first and foremost we are concerned with the development of individuals for whom language is a means to that end, then our scheme of assessment will be concerned fundamentally to perceive that development ("skills" and all) and to further it.

Anyone seeking such a scheme will have to look a long way. If we try to get beyond the traditional examination-type marking scheme rewarding grammar, mechanics, style, content, for example, we find that an immense amount of work has been done on "linguistic" criteria, in which features of syntax and vocabulary are counted. In this way the world has gained the truly amazing knowledge that older children write more, longer, and more complex sentences, and use more words, than do younger ones. It is difficult to see where this gets us. In fact the T-Unit, sentence-combining approach is monumentally unprofitable (except possibly financially), because it dissociates structures from meaning. The work of the London Writing Research Unit (Britton *et al.,* 1975) takes us further, in that it offers us categories for writing which are functional rather than linguistic — a hierarchy of the "transactional." But after all it does not really take us very far. On the one hand the categories are cognitive, saying nothing about other aspects of the personality; on the other they are often very difficult to apply without a procrustean wrenching of the writing to fit them.

It was with considerations like those in mind that the research team on the Crediton Project (Wilkinson, Barnsley, Hanna, Swan, 1980) set about devising criteria of judgment of writing. If we were to be concerned with the writer as a developing being we felt we must be as comprehensive as possible and look at the quality of the thought, of the feeling, and of the moral stance manifested in the writing, as well as the style. Thus we set out to devise models of cognition, affect, morals and style.

Our cognitive scheme looked for fact and statement at the elementary level of writing, and hypothetico-deductive reasoning at the advanced. Slick but myopic critics have said that we were merely taking over the Piagetian model, thus showing themselves sadly unaware that these are working assumptions of the post-Copernican world in which we live. Piaget just happens to have formulated them very powerfully. What alternative formulation would have been preferable our critics have modestly refrained from suggesting.

As for the development of feeling — passionate but steamy authors have written much on this. This field attracts authors whose work is sometimes called "seminal," meaning confused in thought and incomprehensible in language. Certainly we did not understand them and fell back on our own resources, being however greatly helped by the work of Erikson. We saw affective development as being in four directions — towards a greater awareness of the physical and social environment, and towards a mature stance towards the human condition (whilst accepting that one never arrives at "maturity," one is always arriving).

The growth of moral feeling has been much investigated, particularly by Kohlberg from the earliest stage ("I want it, so it is right I should have it" — how well one knows the feeling!) to the later stages based on universal values. But this work does not seem to have been applied to children's writing. We felt it important to do this since we live in a moral world, and are constantly offering explicit precepts to children. (It is interesting to note that young children's literature is full of low-level moral concepts — that virtue is rewarded, for instance, that wood-cutters and aggressive psychopaths like Jack the Giant Killer, are good, and that wolves and old hags are evil.)

As far as "style" is concerned, many examining boards advise their markers to reward it. We thought this meant they knew about it. And indeed some of them do; they act on the assumption that each candidate is called Addison or Steele, and should write accordingly. We could not agree with this, because we came upon candidates called Hemingway and Higgibothem also. And if there is no certainty about style, even less is there any knowledge of the development of style in children's writing. Once again we had to start more or less from scratch.

We therefore offered a hypothesis which cannot be argued in detail here. Briefly, it is that stylistic development in writing is to be seen as a series of choices represented by deviations from the simple affirmative literal sentence so common in young children's writing. Features such as organisation, cohesion, syntax, lexical competence, reader awareness, appropriateness, undergo modification.

The detailed scheme contains about one hundred items. The table contains a simplified version to give the general outlines.

Table 1
The Assessment of Writing

Simplified model based on Wilkinson, A., Barnsley, G., Hanna, P. and Swan, M., **Assessing Language Development** (OUP, 1980)

COGNITIVE Overall Detail	Describing Simple facts, statements	Interpreting Explanations and deductions	Generalizing Summaries, conclusions, classifications	Speculating Substantial hypotheses, arguments, conclusions		
AFFECTIVE	Self Self Self Self	Becoming aware — motives, context, image — of Self Becoming aware of neighbour as self — of Others Becoming aware of, celebrating, physical, social Environment Coming to terms with the human condition — "Reality"				
MORAL Attitudes determined by —	Physical characteristics of results	Rewards and punishments	Social approval	Conventional norms, laws	Motives	Abstract concepts
STYLISTIC	Organisation Cohesion Syntax Lexis Reader Appropriateness	Fragmentary, becomes more and more complete Separate items (e.g. sentences) become cohesive Simple, complex, best suited for purpose General, unqualified uses become exact, chosen Growing sense of reader's needs Movement into more acceptable/efficient mode				

We thus produced a scheme of a comprehensiveness not attempted before. Four models were required because individuals are not necessarily equally developed in all areas. The models enable us to discern this; but they do not produce marks for each feature, and there is no way in which they could produce a single "maturity score." They are intended not as a day-to-day marking scheme but to heighten levels of awareness of features of children's writing. They need to be internalised by detailed study of examples of writing, so that they become part and parcel of teachers' total responses to their pupils' work. The detail of the models enables them to pay due regard to the variety of activity going on in the writing process. As we have said, they are an assessment instrument in the sense that assessment is an essential part of teaching. We need to make assessments of development in order to further development.

The argument this paper began with was that good classroom practice should determine the examinations, and we have been concerned with criteria for making judgments about writing in the classroom. How applicable are these criteria for examinations? This matter has been investigated by Dixon and Stratta who have taken up, as they generously acknowledge, some of the keys ideas of the Crediton Project, and developed them in their work with the Southern Regional Examinations Board in the UK (Dixon and Stratta, 1981). It is clear that, given a liberal examining board and the intelligent co-operation of teachers, there need be no essential clash between at least some of the aims of the classroom and those of the examination. Whether we will ever be able to say the same about graded tests is quite another matter. Indeed many of them exclude writing because it will not lie down and be counted. This is the traditional aim of examiners with language — to get it to lie down and be counted. But language will not do this — it is always up and fighting.

Notes

Britton, J. *et al.,* (1975) **The Development of Writing Abilities,** Macmillan Educational

Dixon, J. and Stratta, L. (1981), **Criteria for Writing in English,**
Discussion Booklet No. 1., Southern Regional Examinations Board

Wilkinson, A., Barnsley, G., Hanna, P., Swan, M. (1980), **Assessing Language Development,** Oxford University Press

A Model for Evaluation in the English Classroom

Ken Watson
Senior Lecturer in Education,
University of Sydney

and

Brian Johnston
Research Officer, South Australian
Dept. of Education

It is stating the obvious to say that English teachers' approaches to the problems of assessment and evaluation have been characterised by uncertainty and confusion. It is often not realised, however, that this uncertainty is communicated to (or perhaps simply shared by) their students. When, a few years ago, over one thousand students in six secondary schools in New South Wales were polled about their attitudes to English, it became clear that some, at least, were conscious of deficiencies in the area of assessment:

> I do not get anything out of compositions where you write something and get back a mark and don't know how you got that mark.

> - Boy, Year 8

> We are told that reading, writing and listening are important parts of English, but we are judged only on how good we are as writers.

> - Girl, Year 9

> What does 6/10 really mean?

> - Boy, Year 9

It is not simply that pupils do not know how they are being judged; they do not know when they are being judged. Lacking that knowledge, they often feel they are being judged every time they open their mouths in class, every time they do any sort of "public" writing (as opposed to private journals). Inevitably, they begin to play safe. They ask questions and offer opinions only when they think that these will be judged "sensible;" they do not voice their difficulties; they are

Figure 1

A Model for Evaluation
in English

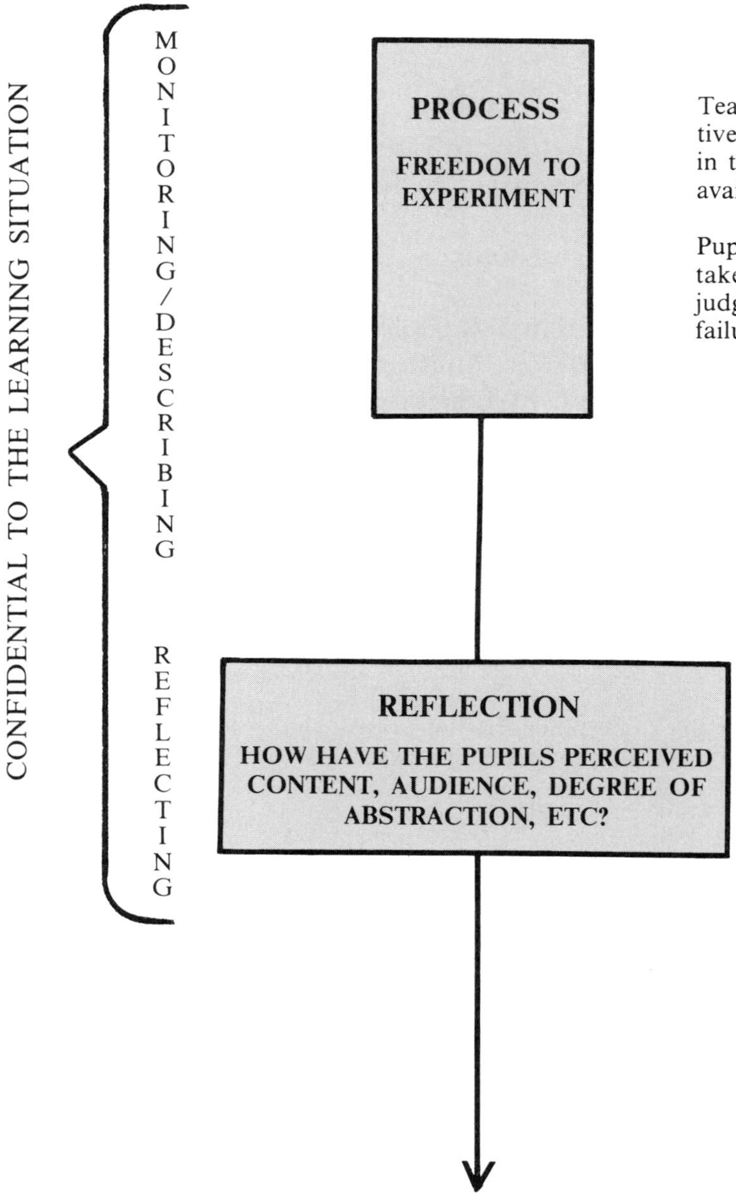

CONFIDENTIAL TO THE LEARNING SITUATION

MONITORING/DESCRIBING

REFLECTING

PROCESS

FREEDOM TO EXPERIMENT

Teacher monitors descriptively to help individuals in their development make available extra resources etc

Pupils must feel free to take risks without being judged on their success or failure.

REFLECTION

HOW HAVE THE PUPILS PERCEIVED CONTENT, AUDIENCE, DEGREE OF ABSTRACTION, ETC?

(cont'd next page)

PRODUCT

E.G., FOLDER OF PUPIL-SELECTED WRITING, CASSETTE, PERFORMANCE OF PLAY, VARIOUS FORMS OF IMAGINATIVE RE-CREATION OF LITERATURE.

Many products will be the subject of appreciation rather than judgment/ assessment. If there is to be grading, pupils should be aware of this and should know the criteria upon which judgment will be made. Pupils should have control over what is presented for judgment.

PROSPECT/RETROSPECT

PUPILS: WHAT HAVE I LEARNED?
TEACHER: WHERE DO I GO FROM HERE?

Pupils should be encouraged to develop skills of self-evaluation. The teacher will have to decide whether to build further upon what has been achieved, or whether a change of direction is needed.

afraid to experiment for fear of making errors. Yet it is often the apparently silly question that reveals where students most need help, and it is often only through risk-taking in speech or writing that children expand their linguistic range. It is very much to be regretted that, at least in Australian schools, the concept of the virtuous error is not widely held — by students or teachers.

These considerations led us to construct a model of evaluation which would guide teachers in their day-to-day work. Most secondary English teachers claim to plan units of varying length for their pupils; this model was designed as one that could be applied to each unit as well as to work over a longer period. We wanted a model which could easily be internalised by teachers, and which would alert them both to the need to base their judgments on sound criteria and to make pupils aware that it is possible for the teacher to adopt, for at least some of the time, a supportive, non-judgmental role.

In the space of a single unit the teacher is called upon to undertake four quite distinct tasks which can be grouped under the heading "evaluation:"

> 1. **monitoring and describing** students' performance in order to help them overcome difficulties and enable them to articulate and understand what they **can** do;
>
> 2. **reflecting** on the progress of the unit: determining, for example, whether the students have perceived content, audience, degree of abstraction in the way originally intended;
>
> 3. **appreciation or judging** the quality of students' products;
>
> 4. **determining,** in the light of both process and product, what should be undertaken next.

Our model demands that teaching be so organised that students know when (1) and (2) are going on and (3) isn't. It urges teachers to recognize that many of the students' experiments and mistakes are a necessary part of the learning process; that such things are confidential to the learning process and not the basis for judging the quality of the student's work. It reminds teachers that it is not necessary that the product of every unit be judged; sometimes it is sufficient that there be appreciation, by teacher and class. It also suggests that an important part of the teacher's role is to encourage the students to develop skills of self-evaluation. See figure 1.

Elements of the Model

1. Monitoring and Describing

Traditionally, teacher feedback aimed at helping the students overcome their difficulties has been confined to comments on the product, particularly the written product. More often than not, such feedback has been decidedly unhelpful. For example, a sample of over 400 marked scripts from eight New South Wales high schools yielded the following data:

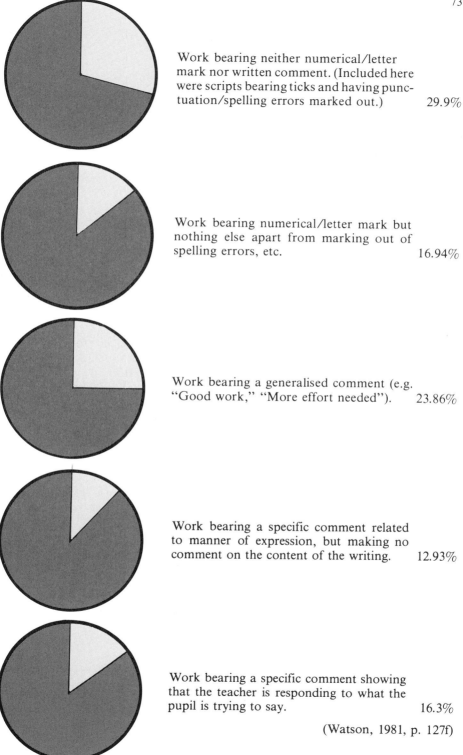

Work bearing neither numerical/letter mark nor written comment. (Included here were scripts bearing ticks and having punctuation/spelling errors marked out.)   29.9%

Work bearing numerical/letter mark but nothing else apart from marking out of spelling errors, etc.   16.94%

Work bearing a generalised comment (e.g. "Good work," "More effort needed").   23.86%

Work bearing a specific comment related to manner of expression, but making no comment on the content of the writing.   12.93%

Work bearing a specific comment showing that the teacher is responding to what the pupil is trying to say.   16.3%

(Watson, 1981, p. 127f)

Similarly, a recent Scottish survey of teachers' written responses to students' essays and poems reported:

> The comments tell the pupil what is wrong or (much less often) right with his performance but, except in relation to rule-governed aspects of English teaching, such as punctuation and spelling, identification of what is wrong or right is in highly generalized, vague terms.

(Research by McAlpine quoted in Brown, 1981)

We must do better than this.

Feedback while work is in progress is essential, but the teacher should not feel obliged always to have to make suggestions for improvement. If suggestions for improvement or diagnosis occur spontaneously to the teacher, naturally he or she will voice them, but it is often sufficient that the teacher dwell on what the student has done, articulating the achievement as clearly as possible. Often articulate recognition alone will help the student more than a welter of suggestions. To take an example, Andrew, a Year 9 boy, wrote the following short piece in class:

> Deep in the dungeons he stands, chained to a cold jagged stone wall. He looks up into the corner to see a tiny hole, where the light shines onto a corner. The light is flickering on off, on off from the gulls. As he watches, the light fades away, slowly until he can see no more.

It is not enough that Andrew leave the class knowing that the teacher liked the piece. At the same time, it is not necessary to give him suggestions for developing it. What is important is that he leave knowing that he has drawn a strong contrast between the freedom of the gulls and the confinement of the dungeon, using the light as a connective device. (Many year 9 students use contrast well, and they can quickly understand the concept when it is applied to their own writing.)

In the case of first-draft writing, Brian Johnston has suggested that the teacher look at the work and ask:

> Do I have a sense of this as a bold statement, a gift? Can I understand why the writer sees this topic as significant? Or do I want more information to let me know how the writer feels about this?

> Where I can see an importance I may not need to do much: just let the student know that I've got the message. . .and indicate the sense of boldness or importance that I get from it. . . .

> My main purpose in these responses is to recognise. . .the power of the students' writing. This can be a dramatic surprise for students who think of themselves as bad writers, and some of them open up quite quickly when they get this recognition.

(Johnston, 1983a)

Similarly, the teacher can monitor small-group discussion by a series of questions aimed at helping the students take stock of what has been achieved at a particular point (something that children often find very difficult to do by themselves). The teacher may respond to talks by highlighting the strong parts or articulating a subjective interpretation in terms of a "centre" and the perceived relation between the parts. Students can also learn to give very simple, powerful feedback to one another.

2. **Reflecting**

This "taking stock" step is a vital part of the model. The dynamic nature of the interaction in the English classroom means that the outcomes may be very different from those intended at the beginning of a unit. The teacher may have altered the direction of the unit because the students have offered suggestions superior to his or her own; the students may have perceived content and level of abstraction in terms quite different from those the teacher had in mind when the unit was planned. If judgments are to be made, they must be made in terms of what actually took place in the course of the unit. In particular, students must not be penalised for a failure of communication that may, in part at least, have been the teacher's fault.

To take an actual example, a teacher designed a unit in which one group in a Year 8 class had to prepare a document describing Sydney's beaches. The teacher conceived this task in terms of factual, expository writing; the students concerned interpreted it in terms of the more emotive language of the travel brochure. As part of the monitoring process, the teacher noted the change of direction and decided not to deflect the pupils from their interpretation. In our model, the teacher, in the course of reflecting on what has gone on, would remind himself that the particular group would have to be judged in terms of their understanding of the task.

In a second example, a teacher reflected on a written task she had set her Year 11 classes on **Macbeth.** At our suggestion she described the task under five headings: content expected, genre, audience, purpose and level of abstraction. As she described the task, she realised that she had not made clear what genre she expected, and that she had not discussed with the students the level of abstraction that was appropriate. She had expected them to show reasoning supported by evidence from the text. But as they were preparing the work, she had encouraged them to express their own opinions of the play. Many of them had done just that, making bold, uncompromising, often naive statements which were genuinely believed and egocentrically expressed with little reference to the play. Clearly, the pieces of writing that resulted could not be taken as evidence that the students were weak in writing about literature, since they had been given no opportunity to internalise the criteria the teacher had been taking for granted. (This taking stock may be — perhaps should be — a joint undertaking of teacher and pupils. Such a joint exploration will not simply sharpen the teacher's understanding of how pupils have perceived the unit; it will also aid the students to develop skills of self-evaluation.)

3. Appreciating/Judging

The products of many units will be the subject of appreciation rather than judgment. The group play or cassette tape, the posters and the collage may be more appropriately the subject of appreciation by teacher and class than the subject of some grading process. Inevitably, however, some products will be judged by the teacher, either in terms of each student's past performance (to see if he or she is developing) or in terms of the student's performance relative to other students. Where either of these two kinds of judgment is to occur, part of the teacher's role in the monitoring and reflecting stages will have been to make sure that students are aware, not only of the fact that such judging will take place, but also of the criteria upon which the judging will be based. Ideally, students should be judged only on aspects of language performance that have been part of the learning process, monitored and reflected upon.

In practice, however, schools' assessment schedules often force teachers to grade or mark students' work before they have internalised the relevant criteria. Because of this, it is most important that students know that judgments are redeemable, that later successes will wipe the slate clean of early disasters. It is shameful that low marks or grades given early in a term or year are often counted in determining the students' final grades; when this happens we are penalising the students for needing teaching! We emphasize that stages one and two of the model, monitoring and reflecting, are confidential to the learning process, and that failed experiments occurring in the process of learning are not to be held against a student when the time for judgment arrives.

Students need to understand that the teacher's role in these first two stages is non-judgmental. It may well be, however, that years of negative reinforcement will defeat the teacher's best efforts to convince students that they are not being judged all the time; that it is possible for the teacher to adopt a non-judgmental role. Furthermore, most teachers admit to giving higher marks to those who follow their advice. In such circumstances, a teacher's suggestions during the process of a unit will assume the status of imperatives; the students will feel that rejection of a teacher's suggestions is a recipe for failure. They will be encouraged to accept the teacher's advice uncritically. Where such attitudes prevail, the only sensible step is to hand the task of judging over to outsiders, that is, other teachers. This has been tried successfully in schools in both Adelaide (Cooke *et al.,* 1982) and Sydney. Teachers report that with this scheme, it becomes a matter of "We will do this" rather than "You will do this." They help students more; the students see the point of redrafting because the work is going to another audience (not the class teacher who has often already understood what they are trying to express); it is up to the students to decide which suggestions of the teacher they will use. The use of external judges has been reported by an American teacher (Burnette, 1980), and the South Australian experiment is currently the subject of detailed evaluation by Brian Johnston.

Where such outside judgment is to occur, the reflecting stage becomes one in which teacher and students discuss the criteria upon which they want the work to be judged. The teacher then has the task of articulating these criteria to the outside judges (a valuable exercise in itself!).

4. Looking Back/Looking Ahead

The final stage in the model is one which encourages both teacher and students to look back over the unit to determine what has been achieved. For the teacher, this retrospective assessment of what has gone on will determine the directions to be taken in the following weeks. How have the students coped with the work? What individual strengths and weaknesses have been revealed? What individual goals might students set themselves? Is consolidation needed in particular areas, or is a change of direction required? (A checklist of experiences to be undertaken during the year is a useful aid at this point, for it helps to ensure balance in the English classroom.)

The degree to which students are involved in this review will depend on how articulately they can describe their work. (The development of this ability is a principal goal of stage one of the model). In some South Australian schools, students are keeping records of what they have been able to do in their written and oral work, as well as examples of work which they consider to show merit, and are formulating goals relating to areas where they plan to experiment. After receiving judgments from an external marker, these students are recording feelings about the judgments and are making statements about future goals, if the judgments stimulate these.

The students are also asked to identify occasions during a unit when they felt excited, anxious or uptight, annoyed or disappointed, satisfied. The teacher suggests that learning is likely to involve all of these feelings. The students are then asked to identify actions they might take themselves, or requests they might have of the teacher or class, which might lead to their gaining more satisfaction from the course and from their own work. These are then discussed, first in small groups and later in the whole-class situation. Of course the approach presupposes that the teacher will listen to the students' requests and attempt to meet them. If the requests contradict the teachers' own requirements, negotiation of a mutually acceptable solution is required in the manner of the "students win/teacher wins" model of **Teacher Effectiveness Training** (Gordon, 1974). Rebellious students often become very involved in this feedback and negotiation process and begin to speak of themselves as serious students of English (Johnston, 1983b).

Conclusion

By identifying four separate roles in the evaluation process, we hope to encourage teachers to give highest priority to **monitoring** students' work. This is a workshop approach to learning where students are not held accountable for their errors: the emphasis is on experimenting, learning from failures and articulately recognising successes.

Secondly, we hope that teacher will **reflect** on the nature of the tasks they set, and recognise that sometimes work which does not match their ideal answer may well be an adequate, even courageous attempt to complete a vaguely defined task.

Thirdly, we hope that teachers will give the students purchase over the judgmental aspect of evaluation by allowing them to select work to be judged and by allowing them to redeem early failures.

Finally, we hope that teachers and students will work together to record each student's strengths and goals for the future work; the aim is that the emphasis be on the positive expectation that the students can learn, rather than an inarticulate labelling of their work on the basis of their supposed abilities.

Our model has been favourably received by many teachers and we are currently preparing detailed reports of how teachers apply it in the classroom. (Johnston, 1983c).

(We would like to acknowledge the help of Edina Eisikovits, Keith Heckenberg, Graham Little and Rosalind Strong in the development of the model).

Notes

Brown, S. (1981) **What do They Know? A Review of Criterion-Referenced Assessment.** Edinburgh: HMSO.

Burnette, P.E. (1980), "Staff grading as an alternative to schizophrenia in composition class," **English Journal** 69, 8, 32-36.

Cooke, J., Cowling, M., Johnston, B., and Manuel, J. (1982), "An evaluation of other teaching grading at Playford High School," **English in Australia,** 59.

Gordon, T. (1974), **TET Teacher Effectiveness Training,** New York: Peter Wynden.

Johnston, B. (1983a), "So Many Good Intentions," forthcoming.

Johnston, B. (1983b), "Student self-assessment in practice: a problem-solving approach to writing," **Developments in English** (forthcoming).

Johnston, B. (1983c) **Assessing English,** Sydney, St Clair.

Watson, K. (1978), **The New English in New South Wales Secondary Schools.** Unpublished thesis, University of Sydney.

Watson, K. (1981), **English Teaching in Perspective,** Sydney: St Clair.

Assessment and the Student

Hayden L. Leaman
Professor, English Education
University of New Brunswick

In the Bay of Fundy fishing village where my boyhood was spent, many kinds of fish were "evaluated" for quantity and quality. Experienced fishermen recognized that different fish at different stages required different measures. We used tubs for mackerel, quarts for scallops, and hogsheads for herring. Although local fishermen accepted the necessity of testing and measuring their catch if they were to be paid, they did not accept the process uncritically. They were well aware that some fish scale buyers deducted ten per cent of gross weight for "water content" even if the scales were already dry. They understood that, in times of glutted market, more of their sardines were likely to be condemned as unfit for human consumption. They knew the Biblical passage, "with what measure ye judge, ye shall be judged."

I have inherited the skepticism of these fishermen about "assessment," but like them I do not reject the necessity, even the desirability, of assessing the product of the labour of a student, a teacher or a school. I simply ask that the measurer, the measure and the method of measuring suit the fish. I ask that those who judge be aware of the effects of their judgments — the impact on teachers and their students. I ask that assessment instruments and procedures be controlled, not in distant research laboratories whose glass walls have never seen a child, but right in the classroom, where the teacher and children are. Perhaps I ask too much.

Let me narrow the field of discussion to "assessment of writing." For a half-century we have been using various so-called "objective tests" for measurement of writing competence. During all that time we have confused detection of error with actual composition in writing — with too little thought about the effect of such tests on teachers, students and classroom teaching. Often we have picked away at trivia until the fish are spoiled and the fisherman discouraged. We have used tests, as fish factories do on the assembly line, to prevent a non-standard product from receiving the official seal of approval and reaching the marketplace.

I would like to compare, if I may, two New Brunswick elementary schools, both faced with the necessity of being able to report how well their students write. (The schools actually exist, but the principals' names have been changed.)

In Charles Foster's school, measurement of writing is done by three means: teacher-made tests, chiefly short answer; tests accompanying the basal reader series; and The Canadian Tests of Basic Skills. Charles is uneasy about all these tests, but has not found an alternative. In all three tests, two of which are used country-wide, he has found items that are incorrect, ambiguous, or invalid for the objective stated. All three, he has discovered, stress error detection and "naming of parts" to the exclusion of selecting and organizing ideas for a purpose and an audience.

Charles Foster knows that the CTBS yields neat numbers which are actually used (informally, of course) to rank-order students, teachers and schools. He also knows that teachers, as you and I would no doubt do, are teaching towards these narrow, inadequate tests, restricting their teaching. Writing is being squeezed out of the classroom. Surprise? Of course not. Tests restrict teachers who, in turn, restrict their students.

Anyone watching the progress of basic skills testing in the United States and Canada is no doubt aware of the extensive basic-competency tests in Florida schools. Probably few are aware of another development in Florida that seems related to the testing. Out of concern for the lack of actual writing in high school classrooms, the Florida State Department of Education makes special grants to schools which can prove that their students write one short composition a week. Possibly Florida students never have written prose paragraphs — or possibly mass testing and fill-in-the-blanks workbooks killed the very practice they were designed to foster.

Faced with tests towards which they feel they must teach, teachers demand matching textbooks. Recently, I reviewed a California-written book, designed for students in business. Its author, in the lengthy preface, pays lip-service to writing for purpose, etc. The four hundred twenty-four page text, however, an entire year's work, rarely asks the student user to write a sentence. And when it does ask, the task is rewriting — to correct mechanial errors. An entire year devoted to proofreading, narrow tests, narrow texts, narrow teaching, narrow. . . .

If you would like a fuller recital of the problems of mass testing, e.g. SAT, read the March, 1983, issue of **Harper's** magazine. David Owen, in a twenty-one page article, "1983, The Last Days of ETS," he says: "Old-fashioned thinkers may wonder whether a multiple-choice test is really a better measure of barbering skills than a haircut is." The same question Charles Foster asks about the would-be tests of writing competence used in his district.

Four miles away from Foster's school is that of Walter Bird. In the Bird school, the principal is equally aware of the inadequacies of short-answer tests for assessing writing and has a system of writing samples. In each student's personal file in the office are writing samples, one for each term the student has been in the school. These samples do not result from any special writing tasks given across the school; they are simply representative pieces of writing selected from each child's production during the term. Whenever a child's progress needs to be discussed, it is possible to look at all the accumulated evidence, up to ten samples for older students — a record of the student's growth in composing competence, extremely revealing to anyone who has developed the ability to judge the many facets of writing.

The Walter Bird type of assessment has a rather different influence on what students are asked to do. Rather than fill in blanks in workbook lines, the students write often and at length. Wholeness, variety, complexity, imagination in writing are encouraged. The emphasis is on production rather than detection.

Since the Walter Bird system does not yield numbers which can be added, averaged, compared, fed into computers, arranged on charts, it may not be popular with school district administrators. It cannot provide a neat index (as SAT scores do) which allows one to declare that general writing competence is improving, or even holding firm — but the school file of writing samples has many advantages for the principal, teacher, parent and, of course, the student, who can look back over his or her writing from grade one and feel a sense of accomplishment.

As former Chief Reader of the New Brunswick Writing Assessment Program, I recognize the virtues of "holistic scoring" for giving a general picture of student writing. I also am aware of the limitations. By itself, one writing sample is insufficient to allow a firm judgment about an individual student. The province-wide assessment produces little information of immediate use to the classroom teacher.

To give more help to the teacher, the 1977 Scorer's Manual included four sample "essays" for each of the writing tasks included at grades five, eight and eleven. Teachers have been using these to give them standards of comparison for their own students' work. Useful.

Also included in the manual are short analyses of each sample essay. These analyses, teachers tell me, are useful because they give a balanced view of each student's writing achievements and failures rather than stressing the faults. But they too do not go far enough. What is necessary is an in-depth analysis of the writing competence of each child in the classroom (a diagnosis, perhaps, if that word did not carry connotations of disease). After diagnosis — or better, "description" — then, each teacher or the language arts supervisor ought to be able to prescribe what writing activities should follow for the child.

But many teachers have had little experience in looking closely at student writing. Consequently, for three years now student teachers in my Process in Composition course at the University of New Brunswick have been doing writing analysis. Each student teacher selects two school pupils, one a competent writer for his or her age, the other a writer with obvious difficulties. Each week I demand an analysis of one piece of writing from each of the two writers. The assignment is simple, but difficult: "Look carefully at the writing and say what you see." My student teachers are encouraged to express opinions, speculate about what they see, compare students. At first most see little and say less in their analyses; but as the weeks go by their analyses grow in length and depth. By the end of term, sixteen or eighteen analyses have accumulated. The student teacher is able to produce comparative case studies of the writing of two rather different writers, far more revealing and useful than any standardized mass test or holistically scored writing sample.

Labour-intensive you may say. Definitely so. Impossible for a practising teacher to do regularly. But a necessary preparation for an assessment system like Walter Bird's — or for anyone who proposes to become a teacher of writing.

When the classroom teacher trained in analysis assesses student writing as Walter Bird does, what is the effect on teaching and on students? Considerable and positive. The writing conference, for example, changes from a potentially distressing or even demoralizing experience for the child to a positive, encouraging one. The teacher is able to talk of content and purpose and audience and style and organization, is able to show what needs to be attended to in subsequent writing, what has been successful in past writings. The teacher is able to be a writing coach. (Student teachers also tell me that analysis of writing samples has helped them understand their own writing processes and to develop more realistic expectations for their own students. Above all, they have learned caution with the nasty red pencil.)

It seems to me one further step is necessary if our assessment of children's writing is going to produce better writers. We must all become better observers of the writing act, understand better the process of composing. Janet Emig and others have shown us one way.

Earlier this year a freshman student, unusually brave, explained to me why his crippled prose does not match his impressive flow of speech. "I'm left-handed," he said, "and I have to **push** a pen." As I watched this nineteen-year old struggle to form letters and words, I understood his problem. Recently, he has been composing on the typewriter and producing some of the best prose in the class.

A word in conclusion. One can evaluate neither fish nor writing by questionnaire. The best-constructed test produced by experts in glass houses cannot match a perceptive and understanding teacher sitting beside the student.

An Analysis of Students' Writing

Hayden Leaman
Professor, English Education
University of New Brunswick

Three samples of written compositions were obtained for each of two grade five students, and were analyzed. Although the classroom teacher was requested to provide samples from a "top" student and a "lower" student, upon close examination the samples were found to be surprisingly similar in abilities shown. Both students wrote stories which flowed smoothly and sequentially, and which were of comparable length. This raises the question of first impressions and teacher subjectivity. If we, as teachers, read a composition once, and form our opinions and evaluations from that one reading, we might be doing the students, and ourselves, an injustice. During the first reading we often tend to notice structural errors such as punctuation, sentence structure, and spelling, but fail to recognize the use of words which are beyond the student's grade-level spelling vocabulary, the attempt to make a story more interesting through the use of descriptive words, or the writing style used by the student. Our first impressions, formed from one reading, may be inaccurate.

Preconceived opinions of a student may also influence us to categorize a student and his or her work as top, average, or low. This author is aware of the teachers' attitudes towards the two students who were selected as "top" and "lower" for this study. The "lower" student is considered to be a troublemaker who would not try to do well, while the "top" student is considered to be polite and eager to do his best. After analyzing these two students' writings, and finding them to be very similar in abilities shown, this author wonders if the teacher's attitudes might have influenced the ratings of the writings rather than the actual evidence in the compositions.

There are both strengths and weaknesses evident in each student's writings. Jason, the "top" student, has a good knowledge of paragraphing. He appears to know that when the topic or time frame changes a new paragraph is needed. This is evidenced by such paragraph starters as "The tunnel was very dark," "The creature gave me a strange type of food," and "Later back at the camp." Included in this paragraphing is the knowledge to indent the first line, and to begin with a capital letter.

In each writing task Jason uses a narrative style. As he tells the story he informs his reader of any details that are necessary to follow the flow of the story. Jason appears to recognize the need for sequential development. In "The Creature," he makes a gradual progression from hiking, to falling in a hole, to meeting a strange creature, to going to the creature's house, and finally, to running home in order to escape being eaten.

Jason has a high spelling success rate in comparison with the number of words he uses. However, his success might be due to the fact that he does not attempt, for the most part, to use difficult words which go beyond a grade five spelling vocabulary. Much of his writing is competent but dull, with a lack of interesting words.

In several instances Jason fails to use conjunctions where they would have been appropriate, and as a result, tends to have numerous short, choppy sentences. This could be a reason for the composition's dullness. In "The Creature" Jason writes, "I looked around and saw strange hieroglyphics on the walls. I got up and hit my head on the ceiling. I made another attempt to get over to the writings." If these sentences had been combined through the use of conjunctions, the overuse of "I" would have been eliminated, and this portion of the story would have read much more smoothly.

In comparison, Bryce, the "lower" student, managed to write more exciting compositions by using descriptive words such as "scorching" and "chilly," as well as words which are beyond a grade five spelling vocabulary such as "expression" and "approximately."

Bryce, however, made many spelling errors. These spelling errors were apparently due, at least in part, to his willingness to risk using difficult and more interesting words. Perhaps too often we mark a composition with the number of spelling errors in mind, and fail to give credit for attempting to use words which are above the spelling level of the student.

Bryce also appears to have a problem spelling words which contain a short "u" sound in the written form of "oth." Some examples of these are "other," "mother" and "brother" for which he writes "outher," "mouther" and "brouther." The reason for this is not immediately clear to me.

The formation of the letter "w" seems to be a consistent problem for Bryce in that he does not add the hook at the end. This misformation causes what appears to be many spelling errors. For example, Bryce writes *"ʯhole"* for "whole", *"ʯas"* for "was", and *"ʯent"* for "went." It is understandable that a student might misform some letters; however, it does cause problems for the reader.

The narrative style of Bryce's stories is coupled with a sequential flow of thoughts such that the reader does not feel lost. There is a gradual progression to a climax, and then an ending. In "Traped *[sic]* in a tomb," Bryce writes from the third person point of view, but finishes by disclosing that the writer of the story is in fact the person whom the story is about. He concludes his story with "The reson *[sic]* I know this is because my name is Timmy." This is an interesting and imaginative way to end a story.

In the composition entitled "The funnyiest *[sic]* thing that ever happened to me," it appears, at least at first, as though Bryce does not recognize a run-on sentence. He writes, "my mouther *[sic]* walked in the house and asked me to take in the groceries for her and I did, then she told me to clean out my shed, then she told me to clean up my room then she told me to wash the dishes." This is a long sentence which could have been divided into two or three sentences. However, it is evident that Bryce knew he had to use some form of punctuation, so perhaps he fully intended this sentence to drag on in order to allow the reader to sense what it was like when his mother kept dragging on with more and more things for him to do. Run-on sentences do not appear to be a problem in the other compositions by Bryce.

It became apparent to me that both students had some difficulties with homonyms. Perhaps the similarity in the sounds of the words caused the students to forget the possibility of there being two different words. They both confused "there" for "their," and Jason used "threw" for "through."

Punctuation also seemed to be a problem for both students. In some cases periods were left out despite the fact that the next word started with a capital letter. For example, Bryce writes "Dinorus [sic] are warm blooed [sic] and most of them eat plants The rest of them ate each outher [sic]." Errors such as this, as well as spelling errors, could be detected in advance by students if proofreading skills were taught and encouraged.

The close examination of other writing by these students raises the question of the type of writing tasks students enjoy. For what appeared to be a research paper the students wrote comparatively little, and for the most part the papers read as if they were copied from a book rather than being an understanding and integration of information. In compositions which appeared to be creative writing tasks, the students wrote relatively more, and with more expressiveness and imagination. Their stories had a natural flow unlike those of the research papers. Perhaps if the students had a combination of experiences such as reading a book, watching a film, and going out into nature, before beginning to write about the research topic, they would have written from a more personal framework and with less "book talk." We should be aware that the amount of personal, emotional, and intellectual involvement of the student in the writing task will affect the quality and quantity of the writing.

While considering the type of writing task, we must also consider the amount of time to be allotted for the composition of the task. If we expect the students to make their best effort we have to make sure that we do not cut the time short, or force the students to hurry in order to finish the task.

Lastly, it became apparent through these samples of children's writings that we should not assess a student's interest or effort on the basis of the number of lines he or she writes. The style of a student's handwriting affects the visible length of a composition. For example, 200 words in Jason's hardwriting covers thirty-three lines, whereas the same number of words in Bryce's handwriting covers twenty-one lines. This again points to the necessity of careful consideration and analysis when assessing student's compositions.

Part Six

Post-Secondary Assessment in English

In addition to what proved to be a focus on writing assessment exclusively, this seminar was strongly interactive. As its chairperson I set out some of the issues as I perceived them, on the basis of experiences in Ontario, particularly, and Roberta Camp then reported extensively on an experimental project in portfolio development by the Educational Testing Service. The two following presentations, by Catharine Keech and John Dixon, were, in part, responses to Roberta Camp's presentation rather than "papers" in the formal sense. The presentations are therefore recorded here in their original order, preceded by portions of my opening remarks concerning the issues as viewed from my perspective.

The commonalities in all presentations were these:

> That "one occasion" tests and examinations, even if these extend well beyond multi-choice items, are not an adequate or fair test of what students can do.

> That it is inevitable that assessment will influence curriculum, but that if the instruments are well chosen (with vigorous teacher participation) and teachers are properly trained in scoring, then that influence is most desirable: on what is taught, on teaching understanding of the writing process, and on the effectiveness and fairness of assessment.

> That much more study is needed of the various writing modes, the effects of the particular topic ("stimulus," "prompt"), and of the various ways in which we assess writing.

And a fourth was implicit:

> If at the secondary/post-secondary junction or anywhere else one is going to make claims about students' ability (or inability) in language, their **writing** must be properly assessed.

Chairperson's Remarks: The State of Affairs (Ontario)

Peter Evans
Ontario Institute for Studies in Education

There is in Canada no common "admission" test in English for post-secondary institutions, though within a number of provinces there is strong pressure from these institutions for a common testing program, a pressure reinforced by "public" concern about standards and accountability. In a study in 1979 by Peter Evans and Dr. Margot Northey (University of Toronto) it was found that, of 22 "community colleges" in Ontario, 21 were using some kind of test or battery of tests of language/reading competence to assist in placing students in English programs. The situation was a total mess: there was certainly no commonality among colleges, badly dated commercial standardized group tests were often used, and "little wonder" home-made tests were developed willy-nilly. The study was undertaken because these colleges claimed to be seeking some commonality, and the report concluded with a number of recommendations for action.

Though fewer universities in Ontario were using admission/post-admission tests, there was clearly a trend towards them. The University of Toronto has recently considered introducing "College Entrance Examination Board"-type examinations; a decision to proceed to develop their own entrance test awaits the outcome of Ministry of Education decisions about end-of-secondary testing. Universities using tests have tended to employ a combination of an internally developed multi-choice language test and, happily, writing. Community colleges often did not include actual student writing in their post-admission testing.

Emphasis on writing as a part of that "post-admission" assessment has increased somewhat through testing packages developed over 1980-83 for, respectively, the Council of Ontario Universities and the Presidents of the Colleges of Applied Arts and Technology. In these, writing is given some pride of place. These are still far from being in universal use and, whatever their strengths as at least common hurdles and as emphasizing writing, they remain single-occasion tests to be written under highly artificial conditions ("day after Labour Day" in crowded gymnasia) with the premium on rapid score turn around. In the development of the CAAT tests, even in the experimental round, community college English staff were unwilling to give the compositions even two scorings to improve reliability.

Though I raise the following questions from an examination of the current confused situation in Ontario, I believe they are universal concerns which must be addressed wherever first language assessment related to admission to post-secondary institutions is contemplated.

Who is intended to benefit, and should the principal beneficiary not be the student?

How, as an alternative to single occasion limited testing, can the individual's ability be represented adequately and fairly?

Is there really any consensus concerning the competences required for entrance to the different levels and programs in post-secondary education?

I concede both the public's right to know what actual achievement levels are for students leaving secondary school and the need of the receiving institution for the kinds of information by which they can fairly judge the kind of educational experience/achievement of would-be entrants and what an 80 from school A really means in comparison with a 70 from school B.

What, then, is the best compromise that can be worked out between competing needs and costs so that all constituencies can reasonably benefit:

i) the public at large with restored confidence that standards are held to and fairly reported?

ii) the English profession with security that teaching need not be confined to a set of prescribed texts or skewed into subtle error chases to beat multi-choice examinations?

iii) the universities and colleges with a clearer knowledge of what marks ''mean'' as precise information for establishing cutting points and scholarship awards?

iv) the student with proper preparation for any external hurdle, guaranteed opportunity to write under humane, sensible conditions, opportunity for an adequate sampling of his or her work to be considered, a reasonable back-up system for reconsideration - a second chance?

The Writing Folder in Post-Secondary Assessment

Roberta Camp
Educational Testing Service

I should describe first of all the context in which we at Educational Testing Service began to think about a new method of assessing writing ability, a method based on a portfolio of writing in which there are several samples of writing. I will try to focus first on the issues that brought us to this development and then get back to what the portfolio looks like.

Our situation is somewhat different from those described in preceding reports on various Canadian, Australian and British assessments. In the United States, we have the Scholastic Aptitude Test. There is probably not much chance of that test disappearing. In fact, our official statement says that something like 1.5 million students take that test every year. The numbers may actually be higher now, and they do not show any great signs of declining, at least in the foreseeable future. Some of the students who are taking the SAT probably ought not to be taking it: the test has a kind of prestige that goes beyond its best range of measurement. That is one of the things that we have as a given: the SAT was a test designed according to classic measurement theory to be independent of curriculum. It was thought, and some people in psychometric circles still think this way, that a test that is related to curriculum might give an unfair advantage to students who participated in one curriculum rather than another. Consequently a test was devised to measure "aptitude." The aptitude versus achievement issue is very complicated, and it has turned out that the test has had more influence on curriculum than anyone would have anticipated. In fact, having grown up in the Midwest, in Illinois, I didn't know what people do in the eastern United States. When I came to ETS and I found out, first of all, how big it was, and secondly, that people took it and the SAT's so seriously, I was somewhat surprised and even shocked. When I began working with faculty committees on our ongoing tests, I found out that a lot of high school teachers had spent a great deal of time teaching their students how to take the SAT. I learned further that the best teachers and probably some good students resented that imposition on curriculum. And of course it didn't take terribly long before other people began to notice the sort of imbalance in curriculum created by the SAT, which had originally been designed to be curriculum free. That, then, was one of the problems we had to deal with.

A second problem that was brought up by our critics was the relatively narrow range of information provided by a test like the SAT. Probably the SAT is one of the most carefully designed tests ever made by human beings; nevertheless, given the limitations of time, it measures a fairly narrow aspect of ability. That is, it doesn't tell us all of the things we would like to know about students; consequently, our critics were saying that students' talents, experiences, and interests were not revealed by the SAT and that in many cases those qualities, particularly for unusual students and disadvantaged students, might have more to do with success in college than the scores on the tests themselves. So, we had come to feel that we needed a broader range of information.

The third given in our context is that a number of schools, especially schools in the East that have a fair amount of prestige, now require students to write essays with their applications to college: sometimes as many as three or four essays. It doesn't take very long in looking at either the essays or the prompts for those essays, in a variety of schools, to discover that it is not entirely clear to students what they are to write. They are not sure who their audiences are, they are not really sure what kind of writing they should do, and the topics themselves, the prompts, are not very carefully defined: the task is often ambiguous. Once that problem became evident, a group of us at ETS decided that we needed to do something to address some of these issues.

When the writing portfolio project was first presented to me, I was a little apprehensive about it because, as a person who has been associated with multiple-choice testing and development of writing samples and holistic scoring, I was worried about getting involved in curriculum. That has been traditionally the kind of thing we have tried to keep clear of at ETS, recognizing the political problems and recognizing also that we are not an institution very popular as a designer or controller of curriculum. However, as talk on the project proceeded, and as I offered more and more of my criticisms, I gradually inherited the project, perhaps because I had criticized it more than anyone else. At this stage it was very easy to criticize because there were all sorts of measurement problems in trying to devise the kind of measures being speculated about; but it began to dawn on me after I had inherited the project that the idea we were kicking around, a portfolio of writing, might be a way of addressing some of the issues I had heard about from teachers of English at numerous conferences. Those were concerns with writing as a process, concerns about including a variety of writing, writing for specific audiences and specific purposes, encouragement of writing across the curriculum, and some attempt to assess writing in situations like those in which students normally write, or at least a little less like those in which students normally write for tests. So I started thinking that maybe this was a chance after all to explore a kind of assessment of writing that was not simply a one-shot impromptu effort by the student. We have used that method in the past in writing samples that went with our tests. (The advanced placement program is an exception: it includes three writing samples, but often they ask for rather similar kinds of writing.)

When we started on the project, the first thing I did was to go back to those teachers who had made all those nasty criticisms of the tests we had been constructing over the years, and said "O.K., now if we have the chance to do something else, what should it look like? What kind of test should it be?" The other thing I did was to go to a number of admissions officers and ask them what they wanted out of those application essays, what kind of information they were looking for. As I put together the answers to these two kinds of questions, it looked to me as if there might be some opportunities for synthesis. The admissions people told me that they wanted to find out first of all what students are like as individuals, what their experiences are in relation to their talents, how they see themselves in relation to other people. They didn't have very specific ideas about how to evoke that kind of information in essays; and indeed some of the schools that gave me lists of the writing prompts, the essay topics, that they perceived as most successful in this regard included prompts that sounded a lot like some of our more successful topics in the assessment of writing. They also told me that they wanted evidence of writing ability. Consequently these seemed to me to constitute an important connection between what admissions officers wanted and what we wanted to measure, a connection I hadn't really expected.

The third kind of information desired by admissions people was a little harder to define. I eventually ended up putting a label on it. I am not sure it is entirely the right label, but they were interested in what might be called "information processing skills:" that is, in trying to see whether students could take apart some information given to them and make sense of it, decide which parts were important, which parts weren't, and then use that information toward some end. The other abilities they wanted to know about might be called problem-solving skills, in the sense of revealing the student's mind at work on an issue or a problem; and, above all, they felt that, if something like this were to be used eventually in placement (the use wasn't clear at that point, and still is not), it would be a great advantage to get away from the kind of impromptu writing that encourages "off the top of the head" thinking.

The original objectives for the writing portfolio project are roughly the following; they are pretty much the Educational Testing Service objectives.

1. To provide a broader range of information about student talents and abilities than is provided by the Scholastic Aptitude Test.

2. To emphasize writing in the secondary/post-secondary transition and thereby compensate for imbalance in secondary school curriculum caused by emphasis on the Scholastic Aptitude Test (which was designed to be independent of curriculum).

3. To provide a more comprehensive and more reliable source of information for admissions (and possibly placement) than is currently provided by applications essays.

After I had gone through the process of gathering information from teachers of writing, from directors of writing programs, and from admissions, we held a meeting in November 1981. For it I prepared a long discussion paper in which I described all of the problems that would need to be addressed in developing such a method of assessment. I also presented that paper to a group of ten teachers of writing and directors of writing programs, some at the secondary level and some at the post-secondary level. One member of the group was also a Director of Admissions who had worked with disadvantaged students.

What happened in that meeting was, I suppose, not anticipated by anyone. I had thought that we would simply go through the issues in a fairly orderly manner and decide that this problem can be solved, that problem cannot, and so forth; and that they would eventually give me an answer to the question I presented to them: "Is this a feasible idea? Should we pursue it? Is it worth our going any further with it?"

Well, the answer was a resounding "Yes, it is worth doing; yes, it ought to be do-able; yes, we can design writing tasks that would provide a fair indication of the range of writing the students actually do and would also provide the right information to admissions." But the whole sense of the direction of the project changed in the process of coming to those answers. This is obvious in the statement of objectives which came out of this meeting:

1. To provide a comprehensive measure of writing ability that would allow secondary school students to demonstrate a wide range of writing experiences.

2. To provide a focus for the improvement of secondary school writing curricula by:

   a) demonstrating the value of writing in assessment;

   b) formulating a set of writing tasks commonly recognized among teachers of writing;

   c) enhancing the professional development of teachers of writing;

   d) providing the instructional and descriptive materials necessary to the integration of the portfolio into existing writing programs;

   e) providing a forum for discussion of writing and writing instruction in which could be developed:

      1. common standards for evaluating writing,

      2. awareness of strengths and weaknesses exhibited by student writers,

      3. a context for curriculum improvement;

3. To facilitate, eventually, the transition from secondary to post-secondary institutions by (a) providing information less subject to distortion than that provided by the current application process and by (b) improving communication between secondary and post-secondary institutions.

There are some things that are comparable: in the first set of objectives we wanted to provide a broader range of information than is in the SAT's; in the language of the group that met in November, 1981, this aim became the provision of a comprehensive measure of writing ability that would allow secondary school students to demonstrate a wide range of writing experiences. In this objective at least we were not too far from where we started.

The second objective was the one that went a little bit crazy. Our original intention was emphasis on writing in the transition from secondary to post-secondary, an attempt to correct the imbalances caused by the SAT. But look at what happened in the second set. That objective has become, in a sense, the most elaborated part of the project, and it is the one that the teachers actually forced me into: the area in which I felt we were in most trouble, the area of getting involved in curriculum. Whereas I had thought curriculum was not the business of ETS or any organization like ETS, the teachers were saying, "Look, this is what needs to be done. You don't have to do it by yourself. If you do it with teachers, you could end up with a fairly decent project."

So, the portfolio now has as one objective the provision of a focus for improving secondary school writing curriculum. Notice that we are no longer just trying to correct an imbalance that we had created; we are trying to improve writing curriculum first of all by emphasizing writing (that is basically what we started with). Secondly, by formulating a set of writing tasks commonly recognized among teachers of writing, we are starting to describe what the existing curricula are, and we are also providing some leads as to where curricula ought to go. Thirdly, we are enhancing the professional development of teachers of writing. That third step became necessary because, if you are going to try to provide a series of writing tasks, they need to be given in classroom situations. Then, in order to make the experience of the student in one classroom comparable to that of the student in another classroom, you need to provide as much information and background to teachers as you can, so that teachers are likely to present the tests in the same way, with the result that the student in teacher A's class gets as good a chance as the student in teacher B's class. There were a couple of ways of approaching this. Once we had started on this path, though, it was almost as if new necessities were created as a result of putting together measurement and writing curriculum.

Secondly, the English group wanted us to provide instructional and descriptive material — instructional in the sense that it would provide a teaching context in which the writing test could be presented and administered, and descriptive in the sense that it would provide information after the assessment about what the essays look like, what is to be done in the future, what the performance means and so forth, information necessary for integrating the portfolio into existing writing programs. The other concern was: What do you do if you design a series of tests based on the best writing instruction that is going on? What do you do about the schools where the instruction is not quite so good? How can you try to provide a comparable experience for those schools? Well, one way of doing it is to provide enough information so that there is at least a bridge. We wouldn't attempt to prescribe how people ought to teach, but we would try to provide some connection between the ways people often teach and the writing tasks that were presented.

Finally, we sought to provide a forum for discussing writing and writing instruction in which would develop common standards for the evaluation of writing, awareness of strengths and weaknesses exhibited by student writers, a sense of patterns of behaviour in writing, and a context for curriculum improvement. Specifically we thought the proposed forum would probably be a two-day conference in which the papers were actually scored by the teachers who had presented the writing tasks in their classes. They would be trained so that they would develop a consensus, a common set of standards, in evaluating papers, and would then evaluate the papers. They would then talk about what they had found in the papers, where students seemed to be doing well, or where they seemed to be doing poorly, and various other patterns they had observed. Part of that session would be an attempt to describe the behaviour they had seen at each of the score levels for each of the writing tasks, so that a paper that got the top score, for example, would be described as exhibiting certain characteristics, competencies, etc., while the paper that got the next highest score would be described as exhibiting certain others, and so forth all the way down. Thus we wanted to get some reasonably specific information even though the method of scoring, as we originally envisaged it, was still subject to a lot of thinking. The method of evaluation would probably be something like a variation of holistic scoring, but we wanted to get a lot more information out of it than a simple holistic score.

Our third objective is like the third one in the original project: to facilitate the transition from secondary to post-secondary institutions by providing information less subject to distortion than current admissions essays, in particular by having students write essays in response to prompts that are a little better designed and are more likely to produce predictable performance, stimuli that are more likely to tempt the students to write the essays themselves rather than have their mothers or older brothers or sisters do some or all of it for them. We wanted also to improve communication between the secondary and post-secondary institutions, thanks to regional conferences in which the papers would be scored. We hoped such conferences would eventually include people from nearby colleges in addition to the secondary school teachers involved in the portfolio program. Then, as standards were articulated and developed in these conferences, secondary people and college people could talk about standards and about students' performance from their own perspective.

You are probably somewhat curious by now about what we projected the sequence of portfolio tasks to be and how we arrived at them. I said earlier that I had talked with a lot of teachers, especially the teachers who had been most persistent in asking me why we tested the way we did. I went back and asked them what varieties of writing they would like to see represented in the portfolio and what aspects of the writing process they thought most important. We developed a rough prototype for the tasks that might be included. We presented it to the group that met in November 1981, who further refined the prototype. They met again in February of 1982 and tried to specify particular writing tasks. In fact, we had three alternate models of sequential writing tasks, and fell into terrible disarray in the second meeting because, even though we all had something in our minds that we were talking about, when it actually came down to talking about particular situations for writing, particular prompts for writing, our ideas were rather different. We had two days of a very dynamic and sometimes frustrating discussion. We did not come out of it with a design for a writing test, but from issues raised in the discussion I knew how some of those tasks might be developed in subsequent months. In my work in going back to the people who had been at that meeting, and in working with other consultants, I eventually was able to devise something that looked like a pretty good sequence of writing tasks.

At this point, my funds were starting to run out and I was concerned that before all of the funds were gone, we should do one more thing in looking at the writing tasks that we hadn't done yet. It seemed to me very important at this point to get a sound theoretical base for the writing tasks. We held another meeting, this time of a small group of prominent teacher-researchers, in which we devised a sequence of portfolio writing tasks:

1. A personal experience paper - narrative/descriptive paper with some expository impulse.

2. An analysis of a literary or a political piece of writing.

3. A persuasive/argumentative paper based on evidence drawn from a case (the subject to provide opportunity for writing across-the-curriculum).

4. A paper of the student's choice in a genre that he or she considers suitable.

5. A letter introducing the portfolio to its reader.

This sequence is still not final; the project is still very much in developmental stages. But it will give us a place to start. I included first of all a narrative-descriptive paper, but one based on personal experience and leading in the direction of expository writing. We knew that in describing the paper this way we ran the risk of getting tangled up in the various taxonomies for writing tasks and kinds of writing, but we felt that multiple labels were necessary to identify the particular kind of writing we wanted. Also, the feeling I had gotten from both admissions officers and directors of freshman writing programs was that simple narrative or descriptive writing in and of itself would probably not provide the kind of information most people wanted. They wanted narrative or descriptive writing used in the service of some expository purpose, even though that purpose need not constitute a very heavy overlay on the narrative/descriptive aspect of the writing task.

The second paper would be an analysis of a literary or a political piece of writing. This paper is a kind of concession to existing curricula and to English teachers' expectations that there should be something to do with literature in a portfolio of writing. But it also provides an opportunity for students to make some choices: If they are much more interested in political issues, say, than they are in literature, then they can show that they are capable of the sort of analysis we expect of people well educated in the humanities. But they need not do so in the context of literature. They can demonstrate their talent for analysis by writing as informed and perceptive citizens.

The third element is a persuasive or argumentative paper based on evidence drawn from a case study. This is the writing task in which we felt we could do most with information processing and thinking through problems. The idea was to present a set of stimulus material on an issue that is not easily resolvable, but is within the range of students' experience and understanding. The pieces in this set would express contradictory perspectives or points of view, and students would be asked to think through the issues and to write a persuasive/argumentative paper.

I should explain that, in each of these writing tasks, there is a series of steps to help students through the writing process. For the personal experience paper, on the first day a passage is presented with a series of discussion questions. On the second day the students do some writing about experiences they have had similar to the experience presented to them in the literary passages of the first day. On the third day they write a draft, building on the best of the sort of partly structured, partly free pre-writing done the day before. On the fourth day they work with other students to get some indication of where they have succeeded and where they have not. On the fifth day they write a final draft with some revision guidelines in mind. In the case of the persuasive or argumentative paper, we are talking about a longer sequence of events, probably closer to two weeks. There are stages of assimilating materials, deciding what information, what material, is most important, deciding what is not important, trying to find one's initial stand on the issues, re-defining that stand, and so forth. The final product, then, is a paper in which the student takes a position that he or she has come to through this process.

The fourth element in the portfolio would be a paper of the student's own choice in a genre that he or she thinks is appropriate. In order to make this a meaningful choice, we have provided some criteria so the students can decide which of their writing seems to them to be best, which pieces seem most representative of them as writers, which pieces of writing complement the other pieces already in the portfolio.

Finally the fifth component would be a letter introducing the portfolio to its readers. This would provide a chance for, and we would provide some guides for, audience analysis. In the course of the project's investigations we had come to recognize that students are often baffled by the business of trying to address an admissions officer when they haven't really the faintest idea of what such a person might be like or be interested in. The audience analysis provides a chance for students to understand the audience to which they must write, and to present themselves as they would like to be seen by that audience.

Right now, the project has been tabled. ETS is looking at all of its projects in the assessment of writing and is trying to decide what our direction ought to be. I think that, whatever happens to this project, there are some implications that ought not to be lost. One of them is that we have drastically changed the model for assessment. Whereas we had talked almost exclusively before about what could be controlled (and we had sometimes controlled assessment at the expense of not measuring lots of messy but interesting things about student behaviour), we have now moved in the direction of giving up some of these controls in favour of getting more of the varied information we now see as necessary. In contrast to most of the assessment situations described in preceding papers, in the U.S. the SAT is still very much a given; so we know that whatever we do with the writing portfolio there will still be that massive, carefully constructed, very similar multiple-choice test to provide an anchor for psychometricians who demand something that is clearly reliable and comparable from the measurement of one student's experience to another's. I am delighted to be on the other end of that kind of testing, to be providing something to complement the SAT, given that it is still very much part of the picture.

I think what we are seeing right now is a change in measurement theory itself, in the beliefs about what measurement should do. With the 1965 Elementary and Secondary Act in the United States, which requires school districts to demonstrate the effect of instruction on their students, as in the push for competency testing in the 70's, I think we learned that it is no longer possible to expect tests to be separable from curriculum. We now see that tests are going to influence curriculum, and that we need to anticipate what the effect will be.

Whether that recognition is expressed in the use of the writing portfolio or in development of other tests, I think it is with us, and is here to stay. The other change I see is that there are people who are calling now for assessment that is based on theory, and assessment that provides a guide to day-to-day curriculum. A few years ago that would have been near to heresy, at least among the people most often associated with the public image of organizations like ETS.

Writing Modes and Writing "Prompts"

Catharine Keech
San Francisco State University

Roberta Camp's presentation was so very interesting from my perspective that I found myself wanting to do no more than respond. When Camp started working on that project, I was one of the very loud voices screaming about the limitations of the one-shot impromptu test as a way of assessing writing. In professional journals, writers were repeatedly saying, "We've got to do more, we have got to do multi-drafts, we've got to do multi-samples, following the British approach." I was excited to hear that as prestigious an operation as ETS, which is so economy-conscious, reliability conscious, was considering such a messy thing. The best thing about it, though, I think, is the underlying change in outlook which Camp defined so well. We have complained for years about the tail wagging the dog. The fact is that teachers teach to the test, and I had begun to say, "Well we just ought to make it a damn good tail:" If it's going to determine our curriculum, let's make a better test. This was the whole argument behind writing samples in the first place, as opposed to indirect measures. To invent a test that is multi-draft is marvellous, and I anticipated an instant response at the school level: on the one hand as a teacher, excited that the testing was going to reflect more of what students could do in their writing; on the other hand, thinking unhappily of days of examining taken away from days of instruction. And, of course, I instantly countered this dialogue in my head: "Yes, but those 'examination' periods are in fact days of instruction."

The Bay Area Writing Project has emphasized the importance of a great deal more in-class writing, pre-writing, peer editing, and so on, as part of a writing program and as a way of getting students to realize that writing is more than just what can be completed the night before. It is not just on tests that students sit down and dash it off and hand it in. When you send an assignment home, students will generally wait until the night before and hope that thunder strikes and something happens. Thus, building into the classroom this agonizing process of writing (which we have come to think of as really using writing to learn, and using the writing process as a way of finding out things) is very often a way to get kids to derive precisely those benefits from their writing. The test, then, can actually become an instructional unit.

The best part of Camp's plan is the continued co-operative link with the teachers who will be using the test. Another exciting part is that ETS, instead of divorcing itself from curriculum, will become actively involved in a two-day interchange, so that the teachers who are actually teaching are designing the test, designing the tasks, choosing and creating these in ways more appropriate to their curriculum, etc.

The same teachers could also be involved in the reading and scoring. I have made a lot of presentations in California to community colleges and high schools whose staff were saying, "What should we do for minimum competency testing?" They were very concerned about reliability and also cost-effectiveness, and they wanted a nice, cheap, multiple-choice test to say these kids can go out on the streets; they're literate. One of my arguments for a writing sample, however scored, was that the actual process of scoring papers, when a group of teachers come together and begin to talk to each other about what's good in this paper and what's weak in that paper, is itself probably one of the most powerful staff development tools and one of the most powerful ways of affecting curriculum positively. I have led many workshops in holistic feature analysis, an approach to writing assessment similar to what the ETS group will have to do eventually. Besides the impressionistic or overall score, we must look at and name what is affecting us in the writing. By breaking out some of those features we are actually able to talk about what things we need to emphasize in our teaching. For example, it may look as if all of our students have wonderful mechanics and fine hand-writing. However, the writing may begin to break down at the sentence level, in that they use narrative paragraph structure with very little sign of internal subordinate sequence or overall coherence. There are numerous features that can be identified, and the search for them and the creation of a scale to analyze them can make a staff acutely aware of things they could be teaching that they aren't teaching, things that perhaps they didn't know could be taught.

In these scoring sessions, teachers who have each gone into the classroom, closeted themselves, and thought suspiciously of that freaky teacher down the hall who wears beads, or the stiff, uptight teacher up the hall who sits her kids in rows, begin to discover that the others have a genuine appreciation of good writing and a genuine sense of what is weak in writing. A new kind of cooperation and respect can thus be developed.

I was thinking of broadening that: knowledge comes on a national scale. I am sure that there are differences in criteria all over my country. That is the problem Peter Evans addresses in his introductory remarks: the teachers give A's in **this** school if the writing is in a flowery style, and the teachers give A's in **that** school if they get a five paragraph essay, all organized in tight little paragraphs. It seems to me, dreaming of an ideal situation, that it would be good to be able to bring teachers together from schools having those different standards and start a dialogue, and then begin to introduce the teachers to some discourse theory and some of the useful distinctions among types of writing, so that they can see that they are each teaching and rewarding different skills. All of these skills are valuable and worth teaching, but we must begin to sort out which it is most important to test.

So I find such a project promising on many levels. I especially like not divorcing testing from the curriculum, accepting that it is inextricably linked, and trying to do more through this association. In my own assessment studies recently, looking particularly at the effects of the task, the way we write the prompt and all the ways students respond, and at how to evaluate what parts of the question made which things happen to the writers, I have been very interested to find at San Francisco State University a Junior English Proficiency exam developed over many years, an exit exam for juniors. The examiners have had to deal with the fact that a great many students who transfer into college out of junior college or community colleges are not sufficiently prepared in writing for graduation. If they graduate from San Francisco State and go out into the community to be told "You can't write," we would have a little credibility gap. The solution was a writing test as a graduation requirement that would screen everyone — those from our own Freshman and Sophomore Composition classes, and those who got this training elsewhere.

Thus, we introduced a Junior English Proficiency Essay Test which had the marvellous effect of binding the staff together. Three times a year, we score hundreds and hundreds of writing samples. In the process of training we recalibrate ourselves in terms of our own standards and what we are trying to teach. Since this whole process had evolved to avoid an impromptu, one shot, event, there is a fallback system; the student's graduation depends on it. If you don't pass, your test is re-analysed and a counsellor talks to you about the weaknesses; if you claim that you were not feeling well that day or the essay was not representative of your writing, you get a retest. If you fail again, you take a Junior English course which essentially makes up the difference, and satisfies the graduation requirement.

What is interesting are the changes to the topics over the years and the quite stringent testing system we have developed for topics. We have developed what we call a **personal experience essay,** which is carefully calculated not to elicit narrative. We want students to have some other organizing principles in their repertoire. We simply take it as a given that all students can in fact structure prose narratively. This is what students learn earliest, they get plenty of practice in it. We need to know whether, when that option is removed, they can generate an extended piece of discourse organized in another fashion. We do want to give them ample opportunity to use what I call "representative prose," which is both description and narration, little summary narratives full of really concrete detail, because we feel that this is an extremely important part of any writing no matter how generalized. If you can tie your generalizations to actual experience, the writing becomes more vivid and comprehensible to the reader, who will realize that you are talking about something that has meaning for you.

But we also want to push students towards showing that they can reflect on experience, comment on it, explain, and use some of the language they need; for example, to evaluate effects. We also know that we are giving them only an hour to write, and they are coming from extremely varied backgrounds. So we cannot make the topic dependent on special knowledge. Accordingly we go for personal subjects: "Everybody has a weakness. What is your weakness? How has it affected your life? What would you like to do about it?" "Everybody has a special talent. Some people are very obviously talented; other people have more subtle talents like ——." We cue very heavily to trigger the invention process instantly. "Everybody has a pet irritation," etc.

We start at this generalized level: "Here is something that is a common human experience. What is your version of this experience? Draw on the concrete details you have immediately accessible, but evaluate, speculate, analyse, explain, etc." We find that these topics are very effective. Some topics push students towards narrative more than others do; but usually we weed these topics out in the pre-testing, and we have found consistently from year to year that the topics tend to work in a fairly similar manner.

The last feature is important when we are talking about criterion-referenced measure. It would not be fair to have a very enabling topic one year and a very disenabling one the next year, when everybody is supposed to be equally able to pass. We find that, with the similarity of topics and the readers being trained each year again and again, we have an incredible reliability rating; we have fewer than 1% discrepancies. That system seems to have worked out.

Now, exactly because tests do affect curriculum, I have found it very interesting to observe their effect on the freshman composition program from my perspectives both as program director and teacher. I have found **myself** affected. The awareness that we want our students to pass and the fact that these test topics have been designed so carefully to do the very kinds of things we would like to have our freshman composition students do (i.e., to draw on personal experience but learn to reflect on it, and push towards analytical exposition) results in a strong tendency to use that type of topic within the program. And I see that test as a minimum proficiency test. It sets a task that can be done in an hour to find out if you are literate, if you can go out in the world and sit down and write your ideas.

However, I find that when our students leave the Freshman English Program and go into the Sophomore English Program, where they are asked to respond to literature, they suddenly bite the dust. The sophomore professors turn to us and say, "Why have you not been teaching them to write?" I respond, "Well I have. Look at this beautiful writing, the spectacular writing, they have done for me." But I do admit that it is very much easier, a very elementary kind of reflection and analysis: it is not a reflection of someone else's language and ideas, but only of direct experience. The "données" are very concrete. Consequently, I have recently begun to analyse a little bit what changes, and, without pushing them toward talking about writing, I have been getting them to investigate ideas and materials other than those instantly available in their own experience. They do this in other courses; they feel cheated if they do not do it in Freshman English. However, when the task becomes difficult, when the primary material that they are working with becomes more difficult, their attention goes to the material, while in Freshman English we are trying to get them to concentrate on their writing: we want them to learn more sophisticated sentence patterns; we want them to think about crafting paragraphs, etc. We must not give them too many things to do at once. So we are really still working out developmentally the things that need to happen first.

There is one last problem. We get a number of students, especially from private schools and the "better" high schools, who have been pushed into fairly high powered and abstract exposition at an early point. Many of these students (I don't know whether it naturally occurs within the student or whether it comes from the teacher's emphasis), have a particular predilection for ten-dollar words. They are very heavy thesaurus users. I think it is wonderful that they are experimenting with words, but somewhere along the line they have been pushed into imitating forms and sounds of language while losing all sense that language is an act of meaningful communication. It is as if somebody sliced at the roots of a plant. Now the flower is in the vase. It is a wonderful flower, but it cannot keep producing; it can do nothing but wilt. I want to go back to the plant, to get these students to go back and get re-rooted in meaning, to see that language should say something meaningful rather than be an imitation of a sound to an easy-to-impress teacher. It's Ken McCrorie's "English," a disease particularly difficult to eradicate. We attack it on a lot of levels. We talk about poor focus, etc. But mostly I find that I hit it by driving these students back to concrete personal experience, by saying: "I don't care if you want to write all this stuff; I want you to write about what you know so that we can talk about your sentences." When they rediscover this capacity, I find that they can move very quickly back to another level.

All minimum competency testing has the effect, unless we actively combat it, of lowering our goals. We need to see that tests address a lower level and to define very carefully for ourselves what beyond that we are trying to do for students.

Writing Modes and Student Response At 17+

John Dixon

Roberta Camp is planning a sequence of portfolio tasks. Leslie Stratta and I have been looking at "folders," as they are called at home, with at best a similar kind of range. These folders are drawn from a year's work between 14 and 16, rather a younger age group.

Our advantage is that the teachers have freedom, in producing the folder, to choose up to (normally) five pieces; you can take the five pieces over four terms, so that you are choosing the best, the optimum achievements, across the range of writing. And you, therefore, are not tied in quite the same way in your teaching. Nor do the students feel, "It's now or never — this is the final chance for me." Because you know that in three terms you will have several attempts at writing of that kind, more process orientation is allowed. It also puts a very interesting pressure on the teacher. You have the whole year to get working with a student. However weak or under-developed he or she is as a writer, surely there is something positive he or she can produce as a personal experience paper; surely there is something positive he or she can produce as a persuasive or argumentative paper, etc.

In other words, both the teachers and the examiners are thinking, "Well now, look, we ought to have something different from the old pass/fail (which we had up to about five years ago as our national system), and different from the definition by deficit of most of the seven "grades." Most of the grades from about grade three have been defined negatively: "You didn't do the things the students in grades A, B and C did; you did less of them and you did them less well." We have actually persuaded all the Examinations Boards that such an approach ought to be abandoned, and that we have to start with definitions, from the seventh grade up, which are positive.

The result is that you now start asking a different sort of question. You start asking, "What is it that makes that the optimum thing that a kid can do; and, if there are other kids whose writing is obviously more complex, what they are producing?" So, while we are studying discourse analysis, as Catharine Keech is, we are actually moving in with a rather different emphasis, I think. We are not looking initially at the linguistic features; but beyond the sentence level, at things like internal events and external events in narrative (inner monologue or dialogue with characterization). These are instances of what you may or may not find in certain kinds of simple narrative. Also we are looking at such features as the point where the selection and the construction of sentences is based on a sense of rhythmic patterning, which gives tensioning and detensioning as your story unfolds. These are very, very interesting to note, and they seem to appear at a certain developmental stage in writing. We are looking now for things that at least hint at very big developmental changes in our students across the whole age range of Sixteen Plus. We have a rather smaller sample to look at, perhaps only half the age group, but by the time they get to Seventeen Plus, we do observe contrast and developmental differences which suggest actual growth patterns between sixteen and seventeen.

The other thing that we are noticing is, of course, how very badly schools, teachers and Examinations Boards have dealt with certain kinds of writing in the past. So instead of writing a book about developmental features in argument, we have to write a booklet about how teaching and argument need to be developed if we are going to get acceptable written arguments. We did that after seminars with the chief examiners involved, looking at written arguments that had come up in course work folders; some of them apparently positive in the eyes of Boards and teachers, but actually with extremely clear negative features. They were not interesting and successful compositions showing the mind at work.

This, then, is the sort of thing we have been doing. It is even more interesting to try to search for development in response to literature. Literary response does involve a development through narrative (and considerably further into narrative, slightly challenging Catharine Keech's point), as well as access into generalized reflective awareness of the human situation in a text. But a full report on these explorations will have to await another occasion.

Wrap Up

At the conclusion of the day, brief oral reports from each seminar were presented to the whole group, and a number of the larger assessment issues were revisited through questions from the audience and responses by various resource persons. The tensions I have attempted to summarize in my introductory essay, "Issues in English Evaluation," were still strongly evident, though strategies for reconciliation appear in many of the presentations, particularly in the areas of writing and post-secondary assessment.

There will be no resolution of the Canadian dilemma surrounding the use of standardized tests until the English profession takes a more informed and more aggressive stance in place of a passive one. CCTE, partly as a result of its 1982 survey of the use of standardized tests, partly as a result of the Montreal experience, has now developed a policy (appended to this volume) concerning evaluation in English in which the use and abuse of standardized tests receives particular attention. The English teaching profession must no longer tolerate naiveté concerning the design of such tests and their statistical properties.

It was appropriate, therefore, that the final speaker of the Montreal preconference session on evaluation in English was a specialist in measurement and evaluation, Bob Wilson of Queen's University, Kingston. He reports being confused at "our" terminology and implies, I think, that a good deal of that confusion is of our own making. Unless we can sort out what we do mean, constructive dialogue becomes difficult, and certainly dialogue and resolution of issues where at present we find a divorce, frequently acrimonious, between the English profession and the measurement specialist becomes impossible. And that is not just a Canadian problem, but an international one.

From the Measurement Perspective, A Word

Bob Wilson
Queen's University, Kingston

When talking and listening to teachers, I have some real difficulty in the use of the terminology that people like me use in our day-to-day activity. I shall share with you some of the difficulty, in the hope that it might illuminate some of the other difficulties you may have had. Point of view in assessment is very important: the point of view of the students, the point of view of the teachers, the point of view of consultants, the point of view of politicians, the point of view of evaluators. These people all come to the task with a number of different ideas about what it is that is to be involved in an assessment. It is important to consider, if we are to understand each other, that each one of these people has a legitimate voice to be heard. Terms like assessment, evaluation, and testing all have different meanings. We can be led to believe that the assessment programs have been equated in some places with standardized testing programs. I think that is wrong; certainly inadequate. There are real differences, and we waste a lot of energy if we do not spend a little time sorting out what these terms mean - evaluators and clients together.

My second point is that assessment, if it is to be useful to program, must be more comprehensive in what it does than merely collecting student achievement data. I know from several programs, British Columbia's being one, that test data collected from students is the least used kind of information that the assessment program has produced. We have to be careful that we do not throw out whatever little babies have been accruing in the bath water just in order to make some political point about testing.

Thirdly, I would say assessment has to be related to the real decisions that are going to be made about programs or curriculum, or we again waste a lot of time. A number of assessment programs have floundered in that they do not really know why it is they are collecting data in the first place. It is not directed at any possible decision. I have a rule of thumb that I would suggest. Take the money that you have available to do the assessment, cut it in half and put half in a bank account to collect interest. At the end of your assessment, take it out and ask,

"Now, what did we find out and what can we do that would be positive education?" Then spend the banked money to do it. One of the problems I have with most assessment programs is that they take more money than can be justified in terms of output that can be attained. We should assess the assessors' results. Another of the things that could be assessed is the morale of the people in the system when they are being assessed. Another is whether the objectives we have for programs are worth attaining in the first place. That is a legitimate assessment question.

My fourth point is that we ought to investigate more thoroughly and in a systematic way the effects of assessment. In the papers presented in this volume there is a lot of talk about the ill effects and the good effects of assessment, but very little reference is made to actual information about how that judgement has been made. We have been involved with trying to follow up some of our assessments by saying, "What actually happened as a result of the reports? What were the actions that were taken?" That is a very interesting activity. There are intended effects, there are unintended effects; there are ill effects, there are good effects. People tend to think only of the extremes: evaluators think very positively about the good effects of assessment; clients think it is the end of the world. Actually, the truth is neither one of those things; but we have to find out what the truth really was. For example, somebody raised the question earlier, if students are asked to create writing samples for assessment, what happens when they do not know the audience for whom the writing is intended? That is one of the principal assessment questions.

Finally, we have a concept of measurement called the standard error. In engineering it is known as the error of tolerance; the idea is that any measure you make of anything is bounded in by a notion that you are wrong, which may itself be a measureable thing. You can measure how likely you are to be wrong, but first you have to admit that you are going to be wrong and that estimates are always going to include an error. That is a **very** healthy notion. It is one that evaluators have to live with. I would urge English teachers, when you talk critically to us, to have a talk with yourselves as well.

Afterword
A Reflective Reaction

Sam Robinson
University of Saskatchewan

The 1983 CCTE preconference session on evaluation, held in conjunction with the annual conference in Montreal, was an exciting time, with reports on Canadian developments as well as reports and comments from Australia, the United Kingdom, and the United States. We ended up dramatically, with the Australians and Britons seemingly rejecting much of the Canadian work in the area of large-scale assessment.

But let me return to the beginning. The first day was given over to a survey of evaluation practices in Canada. Each province reported on its work in the area of large-scale assessment. The provincial representatives were usually Ministry of Education people, reporting at the invitation of Peter Evans, the organizer of the preconference sessions. Given what happened at the conference, as I shall note later, it is important to remember just who was reporting for the Canadian scene, and just what it is that Ministry personnel have to do.

The Canadian reports were followed by commentary and reports from Mike Hayhoe from England, Ken Watson and Garth Boomer from Australia, and Rexford Brown from the National Assessment of Educational Progress in the United States. The English and the Australians politely suggested that they thought the Canadian approach too mechanistic, too given over to looking at pieces of writing and not at writing as a whole. Clausal analysis, T-Unit ratio, error counts — all came in for derisive comment.

This questioning of the "Canadian" approach to evaluation was picked up by John Dixon in his comments at the conclusions of the main CCTE conference. Dixon took an adamant stand against anything mechanistic in evaluation. He categorically stated that any evaluation which does not make for better instruction in the classroom, improving the lives of children, is not worth doing. He backed up his point of view with reference to work which he has been undertaking. He argued for descriptions of growth, with each description being unique to each child. He underscored his point of view by reading to the conference delegates from the works of two students, and asked rhetorically how error counts could possibly make any difference in the writing of these two students. He put forth a compelling argument.

This perspective gathered much support from the Canadian teachers who were at the conference, with a few teachers voicing support from the floor of the conference. But most often, such support came late at night, in the back rooms, during the beer sessions. Here frustrations came out — teachers expressed their secret selves: Ministry of Education activity seems out of touch with the classroom; it is dictatorial, imposed, and downright threatening. The contrasting "humane" position — whether expressed by Dixon, Boomer, Wilkinson, or others — made sense to them at the classroom level.

And so the conference ended: an apparent split in the thinking about evaluation between the Britons and the Australians on one hand and the Canadians on the other, with some mild support from the Americans. Almost a return of Dartmouth, except that the Canadians were there.

RETROSPECT

I am trying to make sense out of what happened in Montreal. Just what is the big question about evaluation anyway? Who has the right answer? What is the right way to go about the process of evaluation? What is truth? And, more disturbing, once we find truth, what do we do about it?

Bothered by these deep-rooted philosophical questions, I began my own search for truth. How does one make sense out of what happened at the Montreal conference?

This quest took me first to my textbooks on curriculum development. I found an answer there, and I would like to share it with you. I do remember that Bob Wilson, a professor of measurement from Queen's University, gave us this answer in his summary at the end of the pre-conference, but no one applied his information to the concerns about evaluation of English in Canada. An understandable omission, since at the end of some twenty hours of hard discussion, conference participants had the strength only to put glass to mouth, and not mind to paper.

Evaluation theory does have something to say to professional organisations like CCTE. Let me try a quick, and perhaps too simple, summary of this area. Evaluation theory indicates, first of all, that evaluation is carried on at several levels: the individual child, the classroom, the school, the system, the district, the region, the province, the country. Indeed, we could even add international evaluation to this list. In addition, there are characteristic audiences for evaluation at each level. The audience for classroom evaluation, for example, is most frequently the student. Although much of the effort at one level may be focussed upon the needs of students, there are other audiences for evaluation information. Parents need information, as do school administrators and school board members. And, at a different level, regional and provincial administrators need data, as do the politicians who are ultimately responsible, in Canada, for the money which runs the school system.

At the same time, each audience tends to receive its data in a specific form. Information which is useful for classroom teachers is best stated in terms of individual students, giving careful descriptions of individual development. Data required at the provincial level, on the other hand, must be broader, reporting trends and general tendencies.

Let me illustrate this point with an example from outside the domain of English: busing students — a big issue on the prairies, with a big budget. Parents want information in terms of their own children — how long will my child ride the bus? Is it comfortable? Safe? Parents, then, need descriptive reports which give a precise feeling for the situation. Our Department of Education bears responsibility for the cost of busing. It needs hard and precise data about the cost per kilometre, or repairs, or safety features — error analysis data is of vital importance.

The ultimate question is not one of right methods or wrong methods. Rather it is the issue of the utilization of information. Certain audiences require definite kinds of data. Indeed, they expect to receive data in certain forms. Politicians who are making hard decisions about costs, and ultimately about class size and student well-being, are not immediately interested in case studies. They do not have time to process this kind of information, nor can they make use of it. Conversely, statistical data are of less use to classroom teachers who are concerned with specific individuals rather than with overall trends.

COMMENTARY

It seems to me that this short summary of the process of evaluation has much to say to English teachers in helping us determine what to do about evaluation. Indeed it should help to make sense out of some of the apparent contradictions that occurred on the floor of the Montreal conference.

In effect, the opposing views of evaluation can be seen, not as contrasting ideologies, but as commentary taken from different perspectives. Let's look first at the position put forth by those concerned with assessment at the provincial level, as reported to us at the invitational session preceding the seminar and in the session on large scale writing assessment by Joyce Matheson from British Columbia, Bryan Roberts from New Brunswick, and Stanley Straw from Manitoba. Their primary interest is large-scale assessment, not specific classroom applications. Their responsibilities take them into trustees' board rooms and even the halls of legislature. In this role, they need finite data, not descriptions of individual cases. To do their job, they are concerned with the identification of the best way to utilize the information that evaluation can provide. They work at a level once or twice removed from the daily operations of the classroom for a special purpose: to give the provincial picture. It is true that their work, the information they provide, can be used politically to convince the public to accept the current state of affairs. This is a problem, indeed a significant concern, but it leads to a different question. The use of large scale assessment data is not evaluation **per se.** But, as Joyce Matheson and Cathy Keech explain and illustrate in their presentations, a cooperative mode in assessment can lead to better practice in the school and the classroom.

Conversely, we have the position developed in various forms by speakers such as Ken Watson, Hayden Leaman and Garth Boomer who demand that the focus of evaluation be the classroom and children in classrooms. Some see little value in the kind of information being collected in large scale assessment, and Boomer in particular perceives it as worse than an intrusion. Error counts came in for some particularly vituperative comment — as illustration, see Andrew Wilkinson's presentation.

Are those responsible at a political level right? Are the others right? Or is there a middle ground — the proverbial Canadian compromise?

It seems to me that the more extreme version of those supporting "humane assessment" could be grossly misleading if not given careful reflection. Their comments on evaluation tend to be limited in scope to only one part of the evaluation process: the classroom. But personnel at the provincial or state level, who have to make vital decisions affecting the classroom, would have a tough time handling the kind of information that an exclusively classroom-centred approach would provide. Descriptions of individual staging points would be mush, something which they could not use to argue their point. This humane perspective, however appealing, is incomplete. It is not one that is totally applicable, for example, to the Canadian context — at least not yet. We Canadians have a definite process by which we make decisions, and the provincial governments play a major role in this process. They need help to do this, hence the appeal of the kinds of information derived from large scale assessment.

Many of the practices necessary in large-scale assessment are rejected too summarily. The kinds of data collected in these surveys are quite possibly the only data which would do the job at the provincial or national level — data which will connect with the audiences for which they are required. Let's look at the possibility of error counts — which many of these critics loathe. This process does have its place in the evaluative scheme of things in the Canadian context. It is quite possible, indeed most likely, that the audience for this information believes that writing may be improved by patching up the grammar errors in written discourse. It is quite possible that data from the various provincial assessments indicate that errors are not a significant factor in measuring writing development. The question then is not whether or not these data should have been collected. It is, rather, how the data are used. I suggest that the data from, for example, the provincial assessment in Manitoba would be more convincing than are "staging points" to the kind of prairie mind which I often confront. Hence, the whole issue comes down to one of utilization — to find the best practices and to use the data effectively.

The world of Canadian education is not black and white, despite what much of the commentary at CCTE '83 seemed to suggest. Yes, we do need the much wider range of evaluation practices. We need some of these "humane" practices desperately — we need the best possible classroom practice that we can develop. The CCTE needs to work hard to make certain that that message is heard and implemented.

At the same time, CCTE should think about the adaptation of such practices for large-scale assessment. Can we, for example, find a way to report students' staging points in language growth to an audience which is unknowing of our jargon at best, and disdainful at worst? Is there a way of representing significant achievement at the classroom level which might complement the overview data which are also necessary? This is a genuine professional question where CCTE and other national organizations must show leadership.

CCTE should continue to look at provincial assessment practices. There is a need to determine what kinds of data are needed and how these data might be reported so that decision makers do have the kind of information they need for the tasks they have to perform. And, if error counts are required, then it is incumbent upon us to find the best way to provide the data and interpret it. We will gain nothing by declaring that this kind of activity is beneath our dignity as teachers.

ENDINGS

Quite obviously our task has not been simplified by the Montreal conference. I have argued in this paper not for a dichotomy of method of evaluation, an acceptance of one position over the other, but for an eclectic approach to the problem so that we might utilize the best information from all perspectives on evaluation. The fundamental issue in this discussion is a sound understanding of what is meant by evaluation. This understanding was not in evidence at the conference. Without it, we will continue to talk at cross purposes and make little progress, to make speeches and sing songs without improving the nature of evaluation one little bit. If we fail to do this, we fail to improve life in classrooms. On this point both the Britons and the Australians would agree with us.

APPENDIX

Evaluation Policy: Canadian Council
of Teachers of English

Proficiency in English or Language Arts is reflected through many aspects of performance and attitude in both expression and reception: through speaking and writing on one hand, and listening, reading, and viewing on the other. It is characterized by habits such as reading and by critical judgment as applied, for example, to literature and to the veracity of information from many sources. Increased enjoyment as well as increased proficiency is an objective of the English progam.

Definitions: In many contexts the terms evaluation and assessment are used almost interchangeably. In this policy statement a distinction is made between evaluation as the activity of making a judgment about worth or value, making a judgement whether performance or program is satisfactory or less than satisfactory, and observations or decisions based upon such judgments; assessment is the process or set of activities by which information is gathered so that an evaluation can be made.

The distinction here is one of convenience, for assessment and evaluation are not wholly separate. The very decision to make, say, spelling performance part of an assessment is a value statement, i.e. that good spelling is important. And the absence of a component such as, e.g., speaking from such an exercise carries the implication, perhaps not desired, that "speaking" is of lesser or little importance.

Evaluation is also, in general usage and here, the term suitable for the total endeavour of conducting various assessments and making judgments.

Principles:

GENERAL:

1. Evaluation, to be appropriate, must reflect in a balanced manner the many dimensions of proficiency; assessment must not be limited to the testing of supposed "discrete" skills.

2. As far as possible, assessment should employ direct rather than indirect measures of achievement, and it may often concern process as well as product.

    Examples: Assessment should be of language in use rather than about usage, language in context rather than through exercises divorced from context.
    Writing assessment should attend to function and audience, and should include drafts as well as final versions.

3. Evaluation should include the reporting of the prevalence of attitudes, habits, and interests.

Examples: The student's breadth of reading interests, participating in classroom discussions, writing interests, frequency of writing both in formal assigments and in self-imaginative experimentation.

4. Evaluation should properly reflect the curriculum: it must be balanced so that all major aspects of the program receive due weight.

Where this balance is not acheived, and performance in relation to a number of "prized" objectives is seldom formally assessed, students will not be slow to draw conclusions about what really matters. Further, assessment skews the curriculum.

CLASSROOM:

5. Students have the right to know the objectives of the program, the means of assessment, and the standards to be met.

Implicit here is the need for a clear statement of program objectives, dialogue with the student, and where possible, informed participation of the student in setting specific learning goals.

The teacher's role in assessment ought not to be exclusively that of final judge or arbiter. In the assessment of writing, for example, the teacher is also the "coach" or "trusted adult" providing helpful response to the student throughout the writing process.

In the design of tests or examinations the teacher should guard against ambiguity or cloudiness, ensure that a good proportion of questions require reflection and judgement rather than mere recall, and provide a marking scheme clearly explicable to student and parent.

6. Parents likewise have the right to know the objectives of the program and, in general, the expectations for the student. They must be properly informed of tests and other measures employed.

7. **The teacher's judgement must be the main determiner of the performance of his/her students, and he/she will employ a variety of measures and observations to inform that judgement. Tests or examinations extrinsic to the classroom should play only a subordinate role in any determination of student achievement.**

Among the measures and strategies teachers may employ are those briefly referred to under earlier policy statements: e.g., surveys of reading attitudes and habits and the examination of earlier and later drafts of writing assignments (writing in process). Teachers should expand the range of assessment strategies, both formal and informal, to include peer and self-assessment. In particular, they should consider the writing folder or folio which may include, in addition to formal records of assignments and achievements, several samples of work from early draft to final product, a selection of the student's best representative work, and, perhaps, some of the student's experimental efforts in a variety of modes that may not have been formally assigned.

EXTERNAL:

(i) Commercial Standardized Tests

The following policy statements in no manner imply endorsation by the Canadian Council of Teachers of English of the use of such products; the statements have been created as advice to teachers and administrators where such tests are in use or their use is under consideration.

8. Any standardized test in use or being considered for use should be rigorously examined by a committee to include teachers responsible for that portion of the

curriculum, with particular attention to **validity, norms, and fairness,** and **use to be made of scores.**

Validity: Among the questions that must be asked are, "Does the test measure important program objectives?" and "Are the particular items and item formats an appropriate way to measure performance?" Further, will use of such a test tend to place more emphasis than is due on particular aspects of the program to the detriment of others?

Norms and fairness: Are the published norms recent and derived from an appropriate population? Should the system develop its own norms to replace the published norms?

Is the test biased against particular groups of students — sex, social class, ethnic background, etc? Do pressures such as mechanics of administration and time militate unfairly against, e.g. thoughtful, careful students?

Use of Test Scores: In what forms are scores to appear, and for what purpose? Have precautions been taken concerning potential misuses such as unfair comparisons of students, classes or teachers? Has provision been made to relate performance reports to program review and revision?

Are individual scores reported to the student, kept in his/her permanent file, used in decisions concerning the student? And are scores so used reported and explained in a manner that takes into reasonable account the standard error of measurement?

9. For all standardized tests or other external tests employed, each teacher, principal or counsellor making use of test data must be acquainted with the basis on which norms were developed and the error of measurement provided in the technical manual for the test, and ensure that scores are reported, used, explained (to parent or student) in a manner that makes clear the limits of precision.

(ii) **Design of External Evaluation: System or Province**

10. Teachers and consultants individually and/or through such bodies within systems as curriculum committees, evaluation committees and, more broadly, through their professional organizations should have a substantial role in selection, development, and the design for administration of instruments, tests or examinations of evaluation at the system or the provincial level. Their role in the general design of the evaluation frame-work, especially the form, scope, distribution of reports, is also essential.

It may be noted in this decalogue that the Policy Statement is intended to emphasize good practice and professional responsibility in general, and is not merely applicable to the English profession in particular. In summary, it calls on the teacher

— *to review carefully his/her own assessment practices*
— *to ensure that evaluation truly reflects the goals of the curriculum*
— *to demand a role in the selection, development and use of assessment instruments.*

*The policy is also intended to draw attention to the entire question of how large scale evaluation in particular can be conducted with greatest benefit (and least harm) to those who should be the principal beneficiaries: the **student** directly, where individual achievement measures may be used in decisions concerning the student, and the **teacher** where design of the evaluation has been such that data can be usefully related to program and to decisions leading to improved program design and pedagogy.*